JEWS

STUFF YOU ALWAYS WANTED TO KNOW
BUT DIDN'T KNOW WHO TO ASK

Dassie Dahan

ISBN-13: 978-1514774465
ISBN-10: 1514774461

Book Layout ©2013 BookDesignTemplates.com
This book is typeset in Gandhi Serif (body text), Amaranth (chapter titles), Gandhi Sans (chapter headings and page headers), and Crimson (table of contents).

JEWS (stuff you always wanted to know but didn't know who to ask)/ Dassie Dahan.—1st ed.

Contents

i

Dedication

Thank you to my family for everything they have done for me.

But most of all, thank You to God.

"Always remember:
Happiness is not a side matter in your spiritual journey.
It is essential!"

Rebbe Naḥman of Breslov (1772-1810)

Who Needs This Book?

The goal of this book is both to give you a taste of what it's like to be Jewish in America and to provide answers to stuff you may have wondered about, like stereotypes and customs.

Although out of necessity, it touches on some Jewish laws and history, its main purpose is to give over the social and cultural experience of being Jewish via facts, statistics, anecdotes, and personal observations (of both mine and others) that represent American Jews of all types: Reform, Conservative, Orthodox, and the unaffiliated—also known as "just Jewish." And even the history presented here is more of a social and cultural history.

So, who is all this for?

Well, maybe you're Jewish, but grew up in a mostly non-Jewish community and you're curious about other Jews.

Or maybe you grew up with lots of other Jews, but you wonder what's going on with the rest of your people in other groups and locales.

Or maybe you aren't Jewish, but you simply want to know what it's like to be Jewish.

Maybe you just want to know the truth behind the stereotypes.

And, Jewish or not, most people want to know whether the Jewish tidbit (particularly if it's a Ḥassidic tidbit) they read in a novel or saw in a movie is true.

Or perhaps you are writing a screenplay or novel that includes a Jewish character and you want to know whether you can maintain authenticity while moving away from the *ad nauseam* stereotype of the dark-eyed, dark-haired, short, upper class, immature, emotional, academic, liberal Jew who speaks with either a Brooklyn or Valley accent, who will date or marry anyone of any race, religion, or gender—as long as they aren't also Jewish—and suffers from workaholic, domineering parents. And let's not forget the neurotic, pushy Jewish mother. (You can move away—far away—from these stereotypes. And the thousands of Jews who don't fit these stereotypes will thank you for it.) Oh, and let's not forget about the portrayals in which the pathetic Jew is finally cured by either hooking up with a bad boy biker or a California beach girl. But they are rarely portrayed as being helped by their own background. In fact, Judaism itself is often portrayed in the same way many people view a profoundly autistic savant—quirky with a flash of genius, but otherwise basically useless.

(I'm not saying that writers should totally stay away from any kind of Jewish stereotype; some of them are based on truth. But one needn't feel limited to them, either.)

The fact is, the stereotypes are confusing because some *are* actually true. As you'll see, most Jews *are* dark-eyed, dark-haired, and shorter than the average American. Yet some stereotypes are based on only an odd grain of truth, while others are based on another group's need to make room for their own theology. If history is written by the winners, then Jews get under history's skin because while Jews have suffered huge losses, not only do they resist total defeat, but Jews also keep making powerful comebacks.

Using This Book

This book was designed to allow you to skip around. So feel free to go wherever your curiosity takes you.

Writing the Book I Wanted to Read—Or Why I Wish There'd Been a Book Like This When I Was Trying to Figure Stuff Out

They always say to write the book you want to read— and that will benefit all the people who want to read a book like that, too. So that's partly what this is all about.

For example, throughout public school, I was always one out of only two or three Jews in the entire school. But I was exposed to a variety of Jews (except Orthodox—I never met one until I was in my teens) via evenings at Hebrew school, youth groups, and synagogue attendance, and I also felt pride in my Jewish identity. Yet the portrayal of my fellow Jews in books and movies often bothered and embarrassed me; I usually felt that they neither reflected me nor the Jews I knew. I also read a ton, but as a Jew, I often felt—with a few exceptions—that there was nothing to read, even in books aimed specifically at Jewish kids. I couldn't relate and my Jewish friends seemed to feel the same.

For instance, most Jews I knew seemed to get along well with both peers and adults. Most are indeed good students and a great many seem to like sports—all unlike the stereotype of the awkward Jewish loner, who was the main character in almost all books I read aimed at a young Jewish readership. In fact, in my discussions with Jewish former nerds and awkward loners, I discovered that they strongly perceived themselves as being different from their fellow *Jews*, whom they perceived as popular and more "with-it." Additionally, many Jews look, act, and talk just like their non-Jewish peers (i.e., they aren't necessarily social misfits with Jewish accents who insert Yiddish slang into every conversation).

Anyway, I always felt that we Jews certainly did not resemble the Jewish characters appearing on film. And I wondered why we didn't.

For example, did I know Jews who were loud and opinionated? Yes. But I also knew many non-Jews who were loud and opinionated—and many Jews who weren't. I couldn't understand why being loud and opinionated was a specifically Jewish stereotype.

Additionally, my community was comprised of many Sefardic Jews (also spelled "Sephardic") with Ladino-speaking grandparents and I naturally assumed that Ladino (Judeo-Spanish) was part of all Sefardic culture (actually, it remains popular with those from the Mediterranean communities of Greece, Turkey, Spain, and the like, but much less so with those Sefardic Jews from North Africa and not at all with those from the Middle East). So despite participating in secular Jewish youth groups and being lovingly forced to attend synagogue regularly, I still didn't have the full picture of my own people, even as I realized that my fellow Jews were more multi-faceted than as shown in movies and books.

Later, as I became interested in Orthodox Judaism, I also had a hard time finding information about what those Jews were like. (This was before the Internet.) Again, movies and TV shows didn't help much. Hassidic Jews sometimes appeared in the background as "color," or else their portrayal was often either negative or just plain foreign. Even during the rare positive portrayal, I was still left wondering if it was accurate. (Mostly not.)

My parents owned a bunch of classic Yiddish fiction translated into English, but I quickly discovered that most of the Yiddish fiction reflected a deep self-hatred, secular idealization, and also a certain ego-absorption (e.g., "What *I* personally experienced in my tiny village in Europe—and later melodramatized in my sick mind—is inherently true of all Jews everywhere for all time who remain connected to Jewish tradition.") Nearly all of the stories featured quasi-Orthodox characters who were ignorant and often behaved in ways that were disturbing, immature, simple-minded, and—as I later discovered—in direct contrast to actual Jewish law. I found it hard to believe that my people had survived and even thrived for millennia, yielding many accomplishments in both the religious and the secular realms, if they and their beliefs and traditions were so deeply flawed. So I decided to continue searching for the truth about Judaism.

Not long after my foray into Yiddish novels, I started to meet actual Orthodox Jews of all stripes and found them to be generally open-minded, compassionate, and intelligent. (Phew!)

More recently, writers of books and screenplays have begun toddling away from the repetitive Jewish characterizations—meaning that now, Hollywood sometimes presents Jews who are physically attractive, cool, and even blonde—but often don't move beyond the other stereotypes. And I'm not even going to touch on the worst Hollywood stereotypes.

But as stated, despite the recent move away from a certain amount of typecasting, Hollywood still repeatedly bombards us with the same narrow characterizations. For example, Jewish characters rarely celebrate Jewish holidays and customs in a way that is beautiful or meaningful—as they are for many Jews around the world. What's more, Jewish characters (particularly on TV and in movies) seldom have a Jewish spouse or Jewish romantic interest, nor are they ever anything but staunch Democrats who express exclusively liberal beliefs. Yes, the above characterization does reflect the majority of American Jews, but why are practically all Jewish characters portrayed this way when there is a significant minority of Jews (46% consider themselves either Republican or Independent, 42% marry fellow Jews, 21% label themselves as right-wing conservatives) that isn't?

"But wait!" you say. "I've seen movies and read books with Ḥassidic characters. And it doesn't fit with everything you just wrote." Unfortunately, these same books and movies are rife with erroneous presentations of Ḥassidic Jews (even if they're positive). For example:

Ḥassidic Jews who carry out graceful, elaborately choreographed dances after a typical Friday night Sabbath meal. (Never happens.)

Or misquoting the Zohar (a book of the profoundly beautiful and secret meanings of the Jewish Bible).

Or the presentation of Orthodox families as stiff and solemn. (With the high Orthodox birth rate, it is hard to be remotely stiff or solemn when you have a truckload of cute kids bouncing around your home—unless, of course, you personally are somewhat uptight and joyless.)

Or homes and study halls filled with poor, somber lighting. (Orthodox homes and study halls are brightly lit; it's easier to function that way.)

Or Orthodox Jews are shown as being fixated on or sorely tempted by the "outside" world. (Many either aren't or aren't in the way portrayed by the book or movie.)

Or a non-Jewish woman forced to cover her hair when dealing with Ḥassidic Jews (no Ḥassid ever expects this and Jewish law doesn't even require it; Jewish law requires Jewish women who have been married or are married to Jewish men to cover their hair; unmarried Jewish women and all non-Jewish women are never expected to do so).

And so on.

This book strives to present an authentic picture of Jews as individuals and to give insight into what the Jewish experience is really like in America.

Yes, this book overwhelmingly describes American Jewry. The Jewish communities outside the USA can be very different and deserve a whole separate presentation.

Clarification #1:

While this book presents a taste of Jewish history and a few superficial explanations of some Jewish practices and beliefs, it does not include a comprehensive rundown due to the great complexity of such a task. (In other words, I want to keep things on the shorter and sweeter side.) Excellent information can be found in many other fine books and online sources. (Suggested resources appear on page 99.) This book focuses more on giving you the greater picture of American Jewry across all denominations from a social standpoint, accompanied by a taste of the actual experience of being Jewish in America, which includes a sense of the complex and contradictory nature of the American Jewish community.

Clarification #2:

When this book discusses Jewish history and tradition, it goes by the majority, meaning the majority of Jews for the majority of Jewish history. For example, most Reform and Conservative Jews believe that the prohibitions against eating pork developed for hygienic reasons, like a fear of trichinosis. True, lessening the risk of trichinosis is a nice side benefit to keeping kosher, but the Jewish beliefs that predate Reform and Conservative Judaism by around 3000 years (as portrayed by 2000 years of rabbinical texts) indicate that keeping kosher is a spiritual discipline and that the consequences of not keeping kosher are mostly intangible. So the information presented here goes by the overwhelming majority of Jewish history and its vast amount of accompanying texts composed by some of Judaism's greatest minds, and not by the relatively recent attempted innovations, although this book does present the views of those newer movements.

So it is true that the majority of Jews for the majority of Judaism's existence believed the keeping kosher derived from spiritual reasons (with some nice hygienic benefits). It is equally true that Conservative and Reform Judaism disagree with this premise and believe that the origins of keeping kosher developed for hygienic reasons.

A Quick Word about Hebrew Pronunciation

As seen from the different spellings of Ḥanukah, Hebrew features a guttural clearing-your-throat sound, often represented in English by *ch*—as seen in the following spelling: Chanukah. This sound is very occasionally spelled as *kh* or *ḥ*. (This book utilizes *ḥ* for the convenience of those unfamiliar with or unable to pronounce this Hebrew sound.)

But there are other inconsistencies you may run into, all due to the different traditions of Hebrew pronunciation. Even among the ancient Twelve Tribes of Israel, there existed minor differences in pronunciation. (This is why you will see the same Hebrew word spelled different ways.) While we no longer know the exact origin of each type of pronunciation, any pronunciation with an ancient chain of tradition is considered legitimate. The pronunciations are split into two main groups: Ashkenazic (Eastern European) and Sefardic (Mediterranean, North African, and Middle Eastern). The biggest difference is regarding the last two letters in the Hebrew alphabet, both called *tav* by Sefardic Jews and both pronounced by them like the letter "t."

However, Ashkenazic tradition labels one *tav* and the other *sav* and pronounces them as "t" and "s" respectively. Yemenite tradition labels the *sav* as *thav* and pronounces it as "th."

This is why you will see, for example, the word meaning "covenant" written as *brit* or *bris* or *brith*. Or the Sabbath written as *Shabbat* or *Shabbos*.

Tav — תּ

Sav/Thav — ת

Today, with the exception of some elderly secular immigrants, only Orthodox Ashkenazic Jews maintain the *sav* pronunciation, and even then, only in prayer, Torah learning, and common terms of speech. All the others (including some Modern Orthodox Ashkenazic Jews) utilize the *tav* pronunciation. When speaking modern Hebrew, speakers utilize only the *tav* and this is the pronunciation used for communication by all, including Ashkenazic Orthodox Jews.

The other big difference is that Ashkenazic Hebrew emphasizes the first syllable of the word (making the word more comfortable to say for English-speakers) while Sefardic Hebrew emphasizes the last syllable. So, for example, the name "David" in the Ashkenazic pronunciation is DUV-id and in the Sefardic pronunciation, it's dah-VEED.

Sabbath, using the Ashkenazic pronunciation: SHAH-bes (Shabbos)

Sabbath, using the Sefardic pronunciation: shah-BAHT (Shabbat)

As you can see, some of the vowels are pronounced differently, too.

In addition, the Hebrew letter represented in English as *tz* or *ts* is pronounced like the *zz* in "pizza" and like the *ts* in "eats." Sometimes, it is spelled with a *z* or even more rarely, an *s*.

And Finally....

Just a quick note—

I try my best to use specific and exact language. Therefore:

"Most" does not mean "all."

"Many" does not necessarily mean "most."

For example, most American Jews (65%) hold a college degree, but not all. Many American Jews (35%) hold a graduate degree.

So yes, 35% indicates a lot of graduate degrees, but it clearly doesn't represent the majority.

DISCLAIMER!

It's impossible to write a book like this without making huge generalizations. I try to be as accurate as possible and to include the exceptions and minorities, but when you're discussing over 5 million people (the Jewish population of America) within such a short book, some are bound to fall between the cracks. For this same reason, there are also very important subjects that I don't cover at all.

And for every thoroughly researched statement I make, you can find at least one Jew who'll say, "That isn't true at all!"

And it isn't—for her. Or him.

To them, I apologize in advance.

CHAPTER ONE

Some Basic Information

Because terms like Torah, Jewish Sabbath, keeping kosher, and matrilineal descent appear throughout this book, it's important to clarify them. And since this is a book specifically about Jews as a people, and not a book on Judaism, my summary below gives only the most superficial description of these intricacies. There are other books and websites that explain Judaism and all its details much more satisfactorily. (See some suggestions on page 99.)

What is "Written Torah" and "Oral Torah"?

Torah

The Torah (also known as "the Written Law" or "the Written Torah") is the Jewish Bible and consists of 24 books, which begins with Genesis and ends with Chronicles II. It was originally written in Hebrew.

Two thousand years of commentaries and texts indicate that Jewish scholars unanimously accepted the first five books of the Torah as having been dictated to Moses by God on Mt. Sinai, then transmitted by Moses to the Jewish people, although God declared the first two of the Ten Commandments directly to the people Himself. The next books were written by various prophets, Ezra the Scribe, and other prominent Jews mentioned in the Torah. Even though the content of the books following the Five Books of Moses were produced through human minds, Jewish tradition always considered these people to have been in a heightened state of Divine inspiration when they produced these works (in some instances, they even indicate a transcription of direct communication with God—otherwise known as prophecy), which enabled accuracy and multi-layered meaning. Jews in every community generally believed this, too, although groups periodically formed that went against this belief, like the Hellenist Jews in ancient Greece and the Jews who joined the Enlightenment in 18th-19th century Europe.

Today, most American Jews are secular and do not believe in either Divine dictation or Divinely inspired composition, and many may have only the most basic familiarity—if that—with the Torah.

Mishna

Originally written in Hebrew, this is an elucidation of the laws written in the Torah and passed down from teacher to student and parent to child for generations.

It is hinted at in the Torah in Deuteronomy 12:21 when it says, "as He commanded you"—yet the Torah itself doesn't describe the command mentioned. That's because a more detailed explanation of this command, along with most other commandments, was given verbally to Moses by God, and not in writing. The Jewish people continued to pass along these elucidations orally, with the Jewish Sages further examining and expounding on them.

With the widening dispersion of the Jewish people, the Sages feared that the vital oral traditions would be lost, so Rabbi Judah the Prince produced a written compilation of the Mishna around 200 CE.

Gemara

> *"Gemara" is used interchangeably with the word "Talmud," although the Talmud is technically the Gemara and Mishna together—also known as "the Oral Law" or "the Oral Torah."*

Written primarily in the ancient Babylonian language of Aramaic, the Gemara is an elucidation of the Mishna. It, too, was an oral tradition accompanied by copious notes on various debates and discussions that went on for 300 years among the leading Sages of that era. An oral chain of tradition kept the discussions alive and flowing and also prevented misunderstandings (because the teacher or learning partner was right there for on-the-spot clarifications). But again, the increasing dispersion of the Jewish people compelled Rabbis Ashi and Ravina to meticulously compile these 300 years of notes into one huge 2711-page book by around 500 CE.

The Talmud is meant to be actively learned with others and is usually studied either with a partner or in a class. It is also studied alone when no partner or class is available. To encourage active learning, the editors of the Talmud strove to preserve the atmosphere of oral discussion within the written form. Therefore, the Talmud uses the same bizarre or entertaining scenarios the original Sages used to keep their students' attention during the lectures and discussions. For this same reason, it also includes purely metaphorical scenarios that can only be properly understood when taught by someone in possession of the chain of traditional understanding (which is what every Orthodox institution of learning does). And to add to the confusion, it also includes one-in-a-million situations that rarely ever happened (in order to allow the elucidation of the law to cover all possible scenarios for all time). In fact, the Talmud may switch between a literal discussion of a topic to an entertaining scenario, then again to a literal discussion, and then to a purely metaphorical parable—all within the same discussion. Furthermore, it is not written in standard formal Aramaic, but as a compilation of extensive notes written in short-hand Aramaic using a distinctly Jewish religious approach. Altogether, this has made accurate translation virtually impossible. Decent translations use copious footnotes, but even the best of these are still sorely lacking.

The Talmud was just not created to be merely read.

It was meant to be studied with an all-encompassing scrutiny and passion.

That is its purpose.

The Jewish Sabbath

Called Shabbat or Shabbos, it is a 25-hour holiday that starts at sundown on Friday and ends when three stars come out on Saturday night. Depending on where one lives in the world, it can start very early in the winter (around 3pm) and end very late in the summer (around 11pm). It is one of the Ten Commandments and Jewish law forbids creative physical labors (as delineated in the Torah and copiously expounded on in rabbinical literature) during this 25-hour period. So for example, Sabbath-observant Jews (called *shomer Shabbat* or *shomer Shabbos*) do not turn on or off lights or appliances during the Sabbath; they either set lights and appliances on a timer or leave them running from before the Sabbath starts. They do not drive or use the telephone or the computer or go shopping. Theoretically, a TV could be left on during this time, but hardly anyone does this because Judaism considers watching TV to detract from the spirit of the day. (And many Orthodox Jews don't even own a TV.) Judaism has always viewed the Sabbath as a gift from God and this time period is meant to be used for prayer, eating especially delicious meals, reading, studying Jewish religion and spirituality, spending time with family and friends, resting, napping, and communing with God. If they live within walking distance of an old-age home or a hospital, Sabbath-observant Jews often take this opportunity to visit the sick and the elderly.

However, Jewish law obligates Jews to disregard the Sabbath prohibitions in life-and-death situations. Meaning, a Sabbath-observant Jew must drive a heart attack victim to the hospital or call an ambulance on the Sabbath, even though driving and using the telephone are normally forbidden. *Not* violating the Sabbath laws in a life-or-death situation is actually a violation of Torah law and considered a *severe* transgression.

Though most Sabbath-observant Jews look forward to the Sabbath all week long, most Jews today either aren't Sabbath-observant or observe only the parts they find personally meaningful and convenient.

Keeping Kosher

Judaism's dietary laws—called *kashrut* (kosh-ROOT) or *kashrus* (KOSH-ress)—are popularly referred to as "keeping kosher." In short, the Torah forbids Jews from consuming blood, pork and most other animal meat, shellfish, fish without fins and scales, birds of prey or any meat from a technically kosher animal that has not been slaughtered and prepared according to Jewish law.

In other words, Jewish law allows for beef, chicken, duck, and venison that has been slaughtered and prepared according to Jewish law. The permissible meat is cleansed from blood via a lengthy soaking-salting-rinsing process. Jews can eat any fish with scales and fins (like trout, tuna, sea bass, and salmon) with no specific slaughtering or preparation process. The kashering procedure used to be done at home, but is now done at a kosher factory. With the exception of some organ meats such as raw liver and heart, all prepackaged kosher-certified meat and poultry comes kashered and ready for cooking.

Combining dairy with meat is forbidden. Jews who keep kosher wait 30 minutes and rinse out their mouth or brush their teeth after eating dairy before eating meat, but wait a longer time after eating meat before eating dairy (usually 6 hours, but German-Jewish tradition mandates a waiting period of 3 hours while Dutch-Jewish tradition mandates only 1 hour).

In life-and-death situations, Jewish law permits Jews to eat anything necessary to stay alive. (This is why, for example, many steadfast yet starving Jews reluctantly ate pork or horse meat during the Holocaust.)

Defining Who is a Jew

The word "Jew" is derived from the name of the tribe of Judah, from which most Jews today are considered to have descended.

Matrilineal Descent

Traditionally, Judaism defines one's Jewishness by the mother.

If the mother is Jewish, then her child is Jewish.

If the mother is not Jewish, then her child is not Jewish.

According to Jewish law, there is no such thing as "half-Jewish"—you either are or you aren't.

The father's status does not define the child's actual Jewishness (or lack thereof) in any way, although a Jewish father's status defines which line of tradition the child follows. (In Biblical times, the child's tribe was defined by the father's tribe. For example, a woman from the tribe of Asher who married a man from the tribe of Efraim would produce Efraimite children.) Today, this means that a family consisting of a Sefardic husband and an Ashkenazic wife follow the Sefardic customs, although in practice, people exercise a lot of flexibility. Many women naturally imbue their home with their family traditions and many children naturally feel drawn to the traditions of their mother's background.

The only other way to become Jewish is to convert.

Conversion

Judaism prohibits the proselytism of non-Jews. (Because Judaism believes that all decent, moral non-Jews will receive their Heavenly reward, then one needn't be Jewish in order to go to Heaven; therefore, Judaism finds no need to try and convert people for their own salvation. See more on page 70.) Jewish law mandates that if someone wants to be Jewish, they need to be rejected three times (as a test of their sincerity and strength of commitment), and undergo an intensive learning program from which they are free to back out of at anytime. It is also important that the potential convert try out life as a Torah-observant Jew to see whether it is what he or she truly wants.

In order to be valid, a Jewish conversion must not be coerced in any way; it must be completely of the convert's own free will. Thus, the convert must not be converting for ulterior or superficial motives, i.e., in order to marry a Jew, or because it sounds like fun, or they just want to be different, or they simply like the idea of being Jewish, or because their Jewish partner's Jewish family members are pressuring them to convert, etc. One who "converts" for such a reason is still not considered Jewish in any way by Jewish law, regardless of what rabbi performed the conversion and what kind of certificate the "convert" received. Most of the laws of conversion are derived from an in-depth analysis of the Book of Ruth.

The only valid motivation for converting:

1) *A sincere desire to join the Jewish people*

2) *The sincere intention to accept upon oneself any and all applicable commandments of the Torah.*

Both of the above are required for any convert. Choosing just one invalidates the conversion.

Up until around fifty years ago, this is how Jewish identity was always defined. Orthodox Jews still uphold these millennia-old laws of conversion. Even so, not all Orthodox conversions are legitimate. For example, some Orthodox rabbis don't really check the potential covert's motives. To the disappointment of some Orthodox converts, their conversion can be rejected by the Orthodox world if the Orthodox rabbi who converted them is known to be careless about his converts' motives and their dedication to Jewish Law.

To avoid problems in the future, any sincere potential convert should check out the sincerity of the rabbi before undergoing conversion and only convert via Orthodox rabbis who exhibit heartfelt dedication to the laws of Torah along with an honest discernment regarding potential converts.

Conservative Jews hold on to the idea of matrilineal descent, but show more flexibility regarding a convert's motives. As far as the convert's intention to actually practice Judaism, this varies from Conservative community to Conservative community. A few Conservative rabbis hold their converts close to the traditional standards expected of converts, while most are much more flexible. Reform rabbis accept the children of non-Jewish mothers as Jewish if the father is Jewish and make few, if any, demands on potential converts regarding actual practice or motives.

Note: Reform and Conservative Jews prefer using the newly coined phrase "Jew-by-choice" when referring to a convert. However, most Orthodox Jews find this phrase inaccurate and offensive because they believe that all Jews should feel they are Jews by choice, whether they were born to a Jewish mother or they converted to Judaism.

CHAPTER 2

Different Groups of Jews

A Brief History

Since the giving of the Torah on Mt. Sinai around 3000 years ago, the overwhelming majority of Jews observed Jewish law in a way that today would be considered "Orthodox." Though it wasn't completely uniform, and different customs and streams of thought developed, the core beliefs and basic adherence to its laws remain the same. For example, all Jews who kept kosher waited a specific amount time after eating, say, a steak. But in Holland, the rabbinically mandated custom was to wait only an hour before having a yogurt. In Germany, the Jews waited three hours. And in the rest of the Jewish world? Six hours. But nobody was eating milk and meat together. Today, Jews who keep kosher still uphold these laws according to their individual origins (although many Jews of German or Dutch origin have taken on the custom of waiting six hours).

The same approach applies to the development of different streams of thought. For example, let's take the practice of astrology. Some prominent Torah Sages considered astrology to be a very real science, yet forbade its practice due to the prohibition from the Torah. Other prominent Sages saw astrology as complete bunk and forbade its practice due to the prohibition from the Torah. So while they differed regarding the actual science behind astrology, both camps still considered the practice of astrology to be both forbidden and harmful.

Ashkenazic and Sefardic Jews

As Jews settled into different areas around the world, different communities developed their own customs and ethnicities.

Today, Jews are generally split into two ethnic groups known as Ashkenazic (commonly called Ashkenazi) and Sefardic (commonly called Sefardi).

"Ashkenaz" was the name of one of Noah's great-grandsons, and the Talmud identifies Ashkenaz's place of settlement as "Germamia," indicating the area of the Germanic tribes. Thus, Jews who settled in Eastern Europe became known as Ashkenazic Jews.

"Sefarad" is the Biblical word generally understood to indicate the Iberian Peninsula and later came to mean Spain in particular. Many Iberian Jews ended up in North Africa and the Middle East after fleeing the Spanish Inquisition, even though there were also non-Spanish Jews in those areas who had arrived after the first destruction of the Jerusalem Temple in 586 BCE.

Thus, Jews in Western Europe, the Mediterranean, North Africa, and the Middle East became known as Sefardic Jews. These terms are standard despite the fact that many Ashkenazic Jewish families lived nowhere near Germany and many Sefardic groups (like Yemenite Jews) never set foot in Spain.

No surveys have been conducted specifically regarding the percentage of Sefardic and Ashkenazic Jews in America. Despite claims that Sefardic Jews represent 30% of the global Jewish population, estimates for the Sefardic percentage of American Jewry weigh in at anywhere from 3% to 14%. But due to their strong connection to Judaism (even secular Sefardic Jews are more likely to celebrate Jewish holidays, send their children to Jewish schools, and attend synagogue than their secular Ashkenazic counterparts), Jewish communities enjoy a far greater Sefardic influence than indicated by such a low percentage. In some communities, Sefardic Jews make up 80% of a synagogue congregation despite representing only 18% of that community.

Large, influential Sefardic communities exist in Brooklyn (predominantly Syrian), Los Angeles (predominantly Iranian), and Seattle (predominantly from Turkey and Rhodes).

Ḥassidism

In 1734, Rabbi Yisrael ben Eliezer became a catalyst for a new-old stream of thought which came to be known as Ḥassidism—called *Ḥassidut* (ḥa-see-DOOT) or *Ḥassidus* (ḥa-SEE-dis), a word which loosely translates as "piety." The ideas on which Rabbi Yisrael ben Eliezer based his teachings remained vibrant in the Jewish communities of the Mediterranean, North Africa, and the Middle East. But due to the false messiah fiasco of Shabtai Tzvi in the 17th century, Eastern European Jewry shied away from the deeper metaphysical practices and concepts based on the Zohar. Hassidism sought to re-introduce these concepts and it spread like fire throughout European Jewry. Some disciples of Rabbi Yisrael ben Eliezer developed into Rebbes, each one emphasizing different aspects of Hassidism. They settled in different areas of Eastern Europe and today, there are over 40 streams of Hassidism still known by their towns of origin. (Karliner Hassidism developed in Karlin, Belarus. Lubavitcher Hassidism originated in the village of Lyubavichi, Russia. Satmar originated in Satu Mare, Romania. Breslov Hassidism originated in Bratslav, Ukraine. And there is even Bostoner Hassidism established in—you guessed it—Boston, Massachusetts in 1915.) But not all Eastern European Jews joined the Hassidic movement. Some even strenuously opposed it at that time. Back then, the non-Hassidic Ashkenazic Jews were called *misnagdim*—opposers—and today they are called Litvaks, a Yiddish word meaning "Lithuanians," Lithuania having been the spiritual hub of Torah learning for the non-Hassidic Orthodox Jews.

Reform

Then came the Reform movement, which established its first temple in Germany in 1815. Reform Judaism leans toward upholding whatever its rabbis consider to be the higher values of the surrounding society. For example, during its development in Germany, Reform leaders banned circumcision, conducted prayers in German only (as opposed to Hebrew), introduced an organ accompaniment to Sabbath prayer services (in light of the prohibition against playing musical instruments on the Jewish Sabbath), observed Sabbath on Sunday (rather than on Saturday), replaced the bar mitzvah (the age of Jewish adulthood, age 13 for boys and age 12 for girls—although many Conservative and Reform communities changed it to 13 for both) celebration with a confirmation ceremony, and rejected the idea of keeping kosher—all of which reflected the values of German society at that time. In keeping with this spirit, American Reform currently advocates the liberal values promoted by the mainstream media in modern American society, even if they directly contradict values clearly stated in the Torah itself.

Today, Reform temples vary greatly in practice. Some conduct an official service that incorporates only select parts of the traditional liturgy in English with some Hebrew and accompanied by an organ. Other temples conduct a more informal service during which, for example, everyone holds hands in a circle and sings Jewish songs, then ends with everyone giving each other hugs and kisses. And so on.

Conservative

Conservative Judaism officially came upon the scene with the founding of United Synagogue of America in 1913, but was really in development for the preceding fifty years. Like the Reform movement, it began with a desire to harmonize Judaism with the surrounding non-Jewish culture (in this case, American), but unlike the Reform movement's founders, the Conservative founders felt a great deal of pride in their Jewish identity and appreciated many core Jewish values and customs. Officially, the Conservative movement believes in God and considers the Torah given by God to Moses on Mt. Sinai (just like Orthodox Jews) and values Jewish law—even though many Conservative Jews themselves do not personally believe this. But in contrast to traditional Jewish belief, they consider the transcribers of the rest of the Bible to be, at best, highly intelligent people of great literary talent, and do not believe the rest of the books to have been written with Divine inspiration.

The Conservative movement considers itself a continuation of traditional Judaism and considers its flexibility regarding Jewish law and belief to be the natural progression of Jewish tradition. However, they define the practice of most laws in opposition to the thoroughly examined opinions of the most brilliant Jewish rabbinical Sages throughout the history of Jewish scholarship. The Conservative movement offers a selection of options it considers acceptable, leading to a wide variation in practice. For example, Jews have traditionally avoided eating non-kosher food or even kosher food that has been cooked with the same utensils as non-kosher food. Jewish rabbinical scholarship was unanimous about this (with the exception of life-and-death situations) for millennia. And this is how Orthodox Jews today still practice. But, for example, some Jews who consider themselves staunchly Conservative eat non-kosher meat at McDonald's while eating only certifiably kosher meat at home. Others eat a McDonald's fish fillet cooked on the same grill as the non-kosher meat, but won't eat the non-kosher meat itself. And still others opt for vegetarian or dairy restaurants only. And some only patronize certified kosher restaurants. Generally, Conservative Jewish communities in the vicinity of large and thriving Orthodox communities (like New York) tend to be more Orthodox in practice. In fact, some may be indistinguishable from some of their Modern Orthodox counterparts (giving rise to the colloquial label "Conservadox"). Those far away from large Orthodox communities tend to be more permissive. Although many Conservative rabbis seem nearly Orthodox in practice, the majority of their congregants often aren't (except for those near thriving Orthodox communities, as mentioned above).

Note: Conservative Judaism shouldn't be confused with political conservatism. Conservative Jews are usually politically and socially liberal.

Orthodox

Before the advent of the Reform movement, Jews did not categorize themselves into formal religious groups. Even the developing Ḥassidic groups represented philosophical differences, not religious ones. Once upon a time, the more religious Jews were simply considered "more religious" or "more meticulous" or "God-fearing" or "those of great faith." And less religious Jews were considered "less religious" or "not terribly meticulous" or "not so God-fearing" or "those of little faith." But all in all, a Jew was a Jew. The lack of a black-and-white labels freed Jews to grow within Judaism according to each one's own individuality.

But when groups of assimilating and then later Reform Jews developed, the rest had to be called *something.* So the word "Orthodox" came into being.

Orthodox Jews live their lives according to the Talmudic interpretations and centuries of rabbinical scholarship that define the practice of the Torah's laws, and thereby consider themselves the authentic continuation of Jewish tradition.

Orthodox Jews are often split into two groups: Modern Orthodox and ultra-Orthodox. But there is a great deal of variety within these two groups and these terms are used loosely. In fact, Orthodox Jews don't even use the word "Orthodox" among themselves.

Modern Orthodox Judaism ranges from people who are very stringent in keeping Jewish law and feel very spiritual to people who are basically secular, but for personal reasons, like to identify themselves as

Orthodox. Modern Orthodox Jews often possess a strong rationalist inclination as supported by their understanding of Maimonides, one of the greatest Torah Sages.

Ultra-Orthodox Judaism always implies stringency with regard to Jewish law. Members of an ultra-Orthodox community who don't behave, look, or think like mainstream ultra-Orthodoxy are considered "more modern" or, if they have rejected significant aspects of Torah law, "off the path."

But again, the labels are unsatisfactory and superficial even in the eyes of Orthodox Jews themselves.

Among themselves, Orthodox Jews rarely refer to themselves as "Orthodox" or "ultra-Orthodox." Instead, they use the word *frum*, which means "religious" in Yiddish. (The *u* in *frum* is pronounced like the *ou* in "should.")

So, for example, in a dialogue between two Orthodox Jews discussing their community, they would not say, "I really enjoy being part of the Orthodox community." They would say, "I really enjoy being part of the *frum* community." The exception might be if someone wants to specify Modern Orthodox. (Modern Orthodox is also shortened to MO, especially in the blogosphere.)

In addition to describing themselves as *frum*, ultra-Orthodox Jews may also describe themselves as "yeshivish." (A *yeshiva* is a place of Torah learning.) In Israel, ultra-Orthodox Jews call themselves ḥaredi (from a Hebrew word meaning to tremble in wondrous awe before God) while all the other

Orthodox Jews generally call themselves *dati* (religious). But Orthodox Jews of all stripes don't describe themselves as Orthodox except when they have no choice, such as when they are speaking with people unfamiliar with *frum* lingo. Also, many Modern Orthodox Jews do not like to think of themselves as "modern;" they feel they are following Jewish tradition as it was meant to be. And ultra-Orthodox Jews do not like the implication that they are overdoing things—being *ultra* Orthodox. They feel they are following Jewish tradition as it was meant to be. Having said that, Orthodox Jews of all types are themselves well aware of the superficiality of the different Orthodox labels and realize that the definitions of what's "modern" and what's "ultra" are often subjective.

Many Orthodox Jews are quite involved in the non-Orthodox world. They attend Ivy League universities and work in non-Jewish offices and live among non-Jewish neighbors—although they will always be within walking distance of an Orthodox synagogue (even if it's a loooooong walk). At the same time, many Orthodox Jews are also very insular and live their whole life within the shelter of their Orthodox community. And between those two extremes lies a wide range of other possibilities.

> **Note:** *Even though they definitely accept Reform, Conservative, and unaffiliated Jews as 100% fellow Jews, Orthodox Jews reject Reform and Conservative conversions along with all the other Reform and Conservative innovations that directly oppose traditional Jewish law and therefore, Orthodox Jews cannot grant these innovations any validity.*

Traditional

This is not an official label, but a colloquial one. These Jews look and act secular, but when they fulfill Jewish precepts, they often do so in an Orthodox manner. For example, they only buy certifiably kosher meat and their bar mitzvahs take place in an Orthodox synagogue. When they attend synagogue services, they do so in an Orthodox synagogue—even if they aren't Sabbath-observant. Orthodox rabbis officiate at their weddings and the wedding contract is written up according to age-old Jewish law. Some live within an Orthodox community, attend an Orthodox synagogue, and send their kids to Orthodox schools, but remain very secular in practice. They may profess a profound belief in God and the Torah's Divinity and express deeply religious feelings. And so on. Many, many Israeli Jews fit this description, although, like in America, this practice is less common among Ashkenazic Jews and more common among Sefardic Jews.

Note: *Conservative Jews often translate their movement into Hebrew as "masorti," which literally means "traditional." But native Hebrew-speakers never understand this as referring to Conservative Jews, but to the traditional Jews as described above. Instead, Conservative Jews are called "Kohnservativy" in Israeli Hebrew.*

CHAPTER THREE

Jews by the Numbers

The following includes some international statistics for comparison.

School

What percentage of Jews attend Jewish schools?

South Africa: 85%
Australia: 65%
England: 60%
Canada: 55%
United States: 23%

Education

65% of American Jews hold a bachelor's degree.
35% hold a graduate degree.

Employment

51% of American Jews work full-time
14% work part-time
(The remaining 35% consists of retirees or stay-at-home spouses/parents or the unemployed.)

Intermarriage

What percentage of Jews have spouses who aren't Jewish?

United States: 58%
England: 43%
Canada: 35%
Australia: 22%
South Africa: 20%

Who's Who in the USA

Reform: 35%
Conservative: 18%
"Just Jewish": 30%
Orthodox: 10%
Other: 6%

Synagogue Membership

Around 60% of American Jews do not belong to a synagogue. The remaining 40% are divided up as follows:

Reform: 39%
Conservative: 33%
Orthodox: 21%
Other: 7%

Beliefs

50% of American Jews believe the Bible is a collection of fables
40% believe it is the inspired word of God
10% believe it is the word of God

Practices of American Jews

72% light Chanukah candles
70% host or attend a Passover Seder (a festive meal held on the first two nights of Passover with symbolic foods and a special reading to commemorate the Exodus from slavery in Egypt)
53% fasted for all of Yom Kippur
23% light Sabbath candles
27% attend synagogue services monthly
22% keep kosher at home

Politics

Democrat: 54%
Independent: 32%
Republican: 14%
––

48% of American Jews consider themselves Liberal/Left-Wing

31% consider themselves Moderate

21% consider themselves Conservative/Right-Wing

Jewish Population

Israel: 5,901,100 (represents 74.3% of the Israeli population)

USA: 5,425,000 Jews (represents 1.74% of the American population)—around half live in New York.

Canada: 375,000 (represents 1.09% of the population)

England: 291,000 (represents 0.47% of the population)

Australia: 112,000 (represents 0.49% of the population)

South Africa: 70,000 (represents 0.14% of the population)

The general American Jewish population is shrinking as around half of Jews intermarry (and the descendants of Jewish fathers and non-Jewish mothers are not Jewish) and because most Jews are now producing less than two children per couple.

However, the Orthodox population is growing. The birth rate among Modern Orthodox Jews in America is over 3 children per family and over 6 for ultra-Orthodox Jews, while less than 3% of Jews who were raised Orthodox marry outside the Jewish faith.

Jewish Geography

Approximately half of American Jews live in New York. In fact, New York contains 15% of the entire world Jewish population. But Miami, Chicago, Passaic, Baltimore, Philadelphia, and Los Angeles also maintain sizable Jewish populations. And while small, there are thriving Jewish communities in places like Providence, Norfolk, and Cleveland.

As far as Jewish immigration goes, Russian Jews have comprised the largest percentage of Jewish immigration to America for the past few decades; they make up around 10% of the American Jewish population. Israeli immigrants are in second place.

Outside of the USA, large Jewish communities are found in Israel, France, Canada, England, Russia, Argentina, Australia, South Africa, and more.

CHAPTER FOUR

Slices of Jewish Life

W hat are some typical anecdotes from the American Jewish experience? The following are experienced by many American Jews.

"Hey, did you know he's Jewish?"

From a young age, Jewish children are taught to identify every famous Jew on their radar. This can be done casually or with great enthusiasm, depending on the Jewish parent's level of passion.

While watching a movie, the Jewish parent (usually the mother) will say, "Hey, did you know that Daniel Radcliffe is Jewish?" The Jewish parent may say this at the beginning of every single one of the Harry Potter films.

Or she might say, "Remember, she's Jewish" every time you watch another episode featuring Kyra

Sedgwick. Hollywood is full of Jewish actors, much to a Jewish mother's delight. A hard-core enthusiast will sit through the credits while her children try to wander off and she'll call out each time she recognizes the name of yet another Jew. Helping a child with history homework is another opportunity for Jewish parents because any historical character who is Jewish will immediately be pointed out.

Even in conversations among adults, the Jewish child overhears:

"Did you hear that Daniel Radcliffe is making another movie?"

"Yes! And did you know he's Jewish?"

Professional sports and the Olympics provide less of an opportunity to identify Jews, but the Jewish mother will give it her best shot and the Jewish father will recall a couple of Jewish baseball players from a few decades ago.

But what if the Jew is infamous?

First the mother says, "Well, maybe [insert notorious Jew's name] just has a Jewish name. Remember David Berkowitz? He was adopted! He wasn't Jewish at all." Later, she'll say in a low, sad voice with an ashamed grimace, "Ohhh...[insert notorious Jew's name] *is* Jewish." And the Jewish father will silently wince. Everyone will seem very uncomfortable for a moment and then they will try to forget about it. Or they will try to find the infamous Jew's good points:

"Yes, Bugsy Siegel was a big mobster, but he donated lots of money to charity."

Entire books are dedicated to the subject of famous Jews. These books basically comprise pages and pages of lists. But many Jews have at least one in their home library.

"Do you know Jeff from Kansas?"

Upon discovering that you're Jewish, someone will at some point say, "You're Jewish? Hey, do you know Jeff from Kansas? He's Jewish, too. I met him last summer when I was visiting my grandparents." Or they'll say, "You're Jewish? You know, I met a Jewish guy from New York. His name was David. Do you know him?" Leading you to answer, "Um, no. There are lots of Jewish guys named David in New York. Like hundreds."

Jews find this both mildly annoying and very funny. In fact, at Jewish youth conventions hosting hundreds of Jewish teenagers from all over Canada and the US, they will at some point bring this up and everyone will share their story (which is basically the same as everyone else's story, except Canadians report being asked if they know Jeff from Vancouver or David from Toronto) and everyone will laugh and feel temporarily bonded by their shared experience.

"How do you pronounce 'Chanukah'? And why is it spelled a different way every time I see it?"

Almost every Jew, regardless of how assimilated, knows how to pronounce Chanukah. That's because their Jewish parent pronounces it properly because his or her Jewish parent pronounced it properly and so on back through the generations....

The guttural sound (like lightly clearing your throat) is often represented in English as *ch*.

There is no English "ch" (like "cheese") in the Hebrew alphabet, so in any transliterated Hebrew word, the *ch* should be pronounced with that guttural sound.

However, because it looks like the typical English "ch" (as in "cheese") and those unfamiliar with Hebrew pronunciation will just find it confusing, many write it with an "H"—Hanukah. In fact, when I write for a Jewish audience, I'll use the *ch* when transliterating Hebrew words. But when I write for a broader audience, I replace it with an "H" or Ḥ– which is why this book writes the word "Chassid" as "Ḥassid."

And for aesthetic reasons, people like to write it with a double-n or a double-k or without an "h" at the end.

"I heard you guys are the Chosen People. What does that mean? Chosen for what?"

This is a great question. It makes a lot of Jews wince. Many Jews haven't thought it through, and feel like they need to try and make up something on the spot. But the deeper reason for the discomfort is because Jews know that they should know the answer to that question. It makes them think and it makes them ponder their role in society, which is a very good thing. Orthodox Jews are generally more aware of what it means, having been taught this by their parents or school, but sometimes in the process of learning to behave "Chosenly," the meaning behind it gets lost.

And the answer? "Chosen" does not imply any racial superiority nor is it a license to act like an unethical jerk. On the contrary, it basically means that one is obligated to be God's emissary of light, goodness, and morality in the world as defined by Torah ethics. Jews are also supposed to increase the knowledge of God in the world.

Judaism recognizes that non-Jews can choose this path, too, by converting to Judaism. Or non-Jews can fulfill their potential on their own outside of Judaism, like Noah and Enoch, who weren't Jewish but are described in the Bible as having "walked with God," which indicates a highly developed level of spirituality and goodness.

"What's that beanie on your head?"

That beanie is most commonly called by its Hebrew name: *kippah* (kee-pah—dome). I know, I know...in books it's always called a *yarmulke* (which in real life, always comes out sounding like "yamaka"), but most Jews call it a *kippah*. Hassids often call it by its Yiddish name: *kopel* (from the Yiddish word *kop*—head). Ultra-Orthodox Jews usually call it a "yamaka." (*Yarmulke* is also Yiddish, but originates from either a similar Polish word or a Hebrew phrase meaning "be in awe of the King.")

Among each other, Jews never call it a "skullcap." Never.

They say, "What happened to your *kippah*?" Or, "That Captain America *kippah* is so cool!"

It is a reminder that God is always above. Many Jewish men who don't normally wear a *kippah* will put one on when learning Torah or praying or making a blessing or participating in a Jewish ritual.

Women don't need to wear a *kippah* because Judaism considers women as possessing enough innate spiritual awareness that they don't need the reminder.

A satin *kippah* in either white, lavender, or blue is popular at Reform and Conservative synagogues during prayer services or weddings.

The finely crocheted and embroidered *kippah* (also called a "knitted *kippah*") is popular among an array of Conservative and Orthodox Jews. The colors and designs on a finely crocheted *kippah* can mean something about the group the guy belongs to, as can the size of the *kippah*. Some boys have their name embroidered in Hebrew or English (or both) on the crocheted *kippah*. The finely crocheted *kippah* comes in a wide variety of colors and designs ranging from a Jewish theme to a geometric pattern to stripes to a Batman theme—and more. Some Orthodox girls crochet *kippahs* as a hobby and pass on their creations to their brothers and cousins and even to their girlfriends' brothers and cousins.

Many Jewish males also favor a black suede *kippah*, a specifically American fashion, making their country of origin immediately identifiable when they visit Israel.

Ultra-Orthodox Jews tend to favor the black velvet *kippah*. Up to a certain age (depending on the custom of the community), ultra-Orthodox boys often wear either a black or navy velvet *kippah* decorated with some kind of embroidery or glue-paint that features the Hebrew alphabet or cars or trains or some kind of symmetrical design.

There are other types of *kippahs*, but this is the main rundown.

"Do you know you're going to Hell?"

Disclaimer: Jews growing up in a more insulated Orthodox environment or in a wholly secular environment do not experience this one or the next.

At some point during a Jewish childhood, a classmate will say, "You're Jewish? Wow. I didn't know that. Did you know you're going to Hell? Yes, you are, too, going to Hell! My parents/pastor said that all Jews are going to Hell because you guys don't believe in Jesus!" This almost always happens only in elementary school, and it is usually said by just one child (usually a girl); all the other Christian classmates have nicer parents and pastors. At that point, the Jewish child goes home and reports this bewildering declaration to his or her parents. The parents then smirk (remember, they went through this, too) and say, "Oh, I know that type. Yep, some people actually believe that." Then, if they *aren't* Orthodox, they will add in a lofty tone, "Jews don't even believe in Hell. It doesn't exist." Another smirk. "Try telling her that." The Jewish child will then dutifully confront the offending child and say (if not Orthodox), "Guess what? We don't even *believe* in Hell. So *there!*" And the offending Christian child will stare speechlessly with a scandalized look on her face.

Sometimes, another Christian classmate (also usually a girl) will come to the Jewish classmate's defense, quoting her own pastor, who preaches a much friendlier view of Jews and their Afterlife.

Note: Judaism actually believes very strongly in Heaven, Hell—and reincarnation, for that matter—but Judaism defines Heaven and Hell differently than other religions. There are 2000 years of texts and responsa on the subject of the Afterlife, referring to it as "The World to Come" or "The World of Truth." Orthodox Jews use these terms in Hebrew and this subject comes up regularly. Yet Conservative and Reform Jews are generally ignorant of it and deny it. I have no explanation for this discrepancy.

"Do you guys worship Satan?"

This question is not funny. It gives Jews the heebie-jeebies and makes Jews wonder where in the world you got that idea from. And as the millennia-old promoters of monotheism, Jews also find it incredibly ignorant and offensive.

Jews Over 45 vs. Jews Under 45

The following contains even broader and more superficial generalizations than the rest of the book and there are certainly many exceptions to what is written here.

The Big Generation Gap

The vast majority of American Jews since WWII has been liberal and voted Democrat. (Orthodox Jews are the exception and tend to be fiscally and socially conservative and vote for whichever candidates support the agendas most in line with Torah values; they tend to firmly support traditional family values.) American Jews tend to put themselves on the front lines of the liberal agenda in every generation. Unless Orthodox, they tend to believe wholeheartedly in the right to abortion at will, gay marriage, and so on. Quite a few are vegetarians or vegans. A great many pride themselves on being well-informed about their positions on the issues of the day. Reform and Conservative Hebrew schools and youth groups will hold classroom debates to educate their students on a variety of issues, and while they'll present the both sides, a strong emphasis is placed on the "correct" opinion (the liberal one). Orthodox schools and youth groups may do the same, emphasizing the correctness of the opinion that most closely reflect traditional Jewish sources (usually the right-wing conservative opinion). Because American society has moved Left over time, the liberal Jews of the Fifties and Sixties find themselves considered not liberal enough by their even more liberal children and grandchildren. Ideals they held to be incontestable (like support for Israel) may be derided by their offspring.

Which leads us to the biggest difference between the over-45s and the under-45s: Israel.

Many Jews under 45 sympathize with the Palestinians and believe the Palestinian-sympathetic rhetoric presented in the mainstream media and generally consider Fatah to be a moderate freedom-fighting organization. Some even consider Hamas to be a freedom-fighting organization. Jews over 45 generally consider both Fatah and Hamas to be terrorist organizations due to the many genocidal declarations and acts of terror they have committed against Jews. Jews over 45 either vehemently oppose a two-State solution or support it only on the condition that Israel's security is completely guaranteed and strictly enforced. Jews under 45 tend to support a two-State solution—period.

Jews over 45 are often proud of Israel while Jews under 45 are increasingly ashamed of Israel. The general exception to this is Orthodox Jews who, regardless of age, tend to think like the over-45 group.

CHAPTER FIVE

Stereotype Busters

"That's Funny, You Don't <u>Look</u> Jewish...."

As mentioned in the Introduction, decades of books (often written by Jews themselves) have often featured Jewish characters who are dark-haired, dark-eyed and are either overweight or skinny late-developers. And short. With bad "Brillo" hair. And possibly, a prominent nose. Interestingly, these characters often hold a strong physical resemblance to their creators.

The Jewish readers (meaning, the majority) who do not resemble the oft-depicted short, Brillo-haired, unattractive, fat/scrawny misfit dislike reading about such characters. They tend to feel embarrassed about being portrayed so unappealingly (because they know that most of their Jewish friends, relatives, and selves do not look or act that).

One of the many reasons for the enduring popularity among Jews of the *All-of-a-Kind Family* series (written by Sydney Taylor between 1951-1978), which portrayed Taylor's Jewish family in New York at the turn of the 20th century, was the appealing and realistic appearance and behavior of this family. The parents were attractive, genteel, kind-hearted people and three out of their six children were blue-eyed blondes. But even the short, dark-haired, dark-eyed ones were still attractive and appealing. Not only could we relate to this family who, like us, looked and behaved within the wide range of "normal" (none of whom were neurotic or guilt-ridden), they were good, kind, intelligent, attractive, talented people with whom we could be proud to be associated.

Hair

An old study featured in the Jewish Encyclopedia (sorry, I found no recent study of this topic) of New York Jews showed that 6% were blonde and 3% were redheads. The rest were some form of brunette, with hair ranging from light brown to black. Only 7% suffered from the stereotypical frizzy "Brillo" hair; most had straight hair, but many did have curly hair.

Sefardic Jews are more likely to be dark-haired (and darker-complexioned), but you can still find natural blondes among them. In my experience, there are more redheads than blondes among Sefardic Jews, but both hair colors are still much less common than they are among Ashkenazic Jews.

Eyes

That same study found that over half had dark eyes and just under half had light eyes (gray, green, or blue).

You'll find Sefardic Jews with blue or green eyes more often than you'd expect, though not as frequently as found among Ashkenazic Jews.

Freckles

Freckles aren't common among Jews, but even so, every Jew knows at least two freckle-faced Jews.

Nose

Only 14% of Jews surveyed possessed the caricature hooked nose.

Height

Various studies have found that Jews tend to be an inch or two shorter than average in whatever culture they live. So I guess we are mostly shorter than your average American. But some Jews are still quite tall.

Weight

I could not find weight statistics on the Jewish community. But my experience is that Jews are about the same weight as whatever their surrounding culture is. Average Jewish weight has probably gone up along with the weight of the rest of America.

Race and Ethnicity

The vast of majority of Jews are white and this includes the Middle Eastern and Mediterranean ethnicities.

Ethiopian Jews are usually as dark as other Ethiopians, but their features are still different than those of non-Jewish Ethiopians. (So the stereotype about "looking Jewish" appears to be true among Ethiopian Jews.)

The black Jewish community is more varied than most people realize. Most black Jews are converts to Judaism, but some are the children of a mixed-race relationship (i.e., a white Jewish mother and a black non-Jewish father) or the children of black converts. Ahuva Grey, a black convert to Judaism, chronicles her journey in her book, *My Sister, the Jew*, which became a best-seller in the Orthodox community. A former prince of Swaziland, Rabbi Natan Gamedze, lectures throughout Israel and America in Hebrew and English and has been interviewed several times.

You can also find Hispanic Jews—sometimes large groups of them. Many of them are converts who recently discovered that they can trace at least some of their ancestry back to the "secret" Jews who originally started hiding their Judaism during the Spanish Inquisition. But because they have no proof of Jewishness, such as a kosher marriage document from way-back-when, they must undergo a conversion. Many interviews with them can be found in the Orthodox media.

Pacific Asian is one of the rarest races found among Jews. (A friend of mine born to a white Jewish mother and a non-Jewish Japanese father jokingly calls herself "Jewpanese.") They are almost always converts. Devorah Goldstein, a Chinese Jew, is the most well-known of Pacific Asian Jews because her father, Avraham Schwartzbaum, wrote a book about adopting and raising her called *The Bamboo Cradle*.

Another minority within the minority are Native American Jews. Avi Shafran wrote the biography of a Mohawk-Naragansett convert to Judaism in the book, *Migrant Soul*.

But again, a person's Jewishness is defined by their mother. That's why a person can be, say, three-fourths Cherokee and still be one-hundred percent Jewish by birth.

Jews are Smart and Rich and Successful

Not surprisingly, Jews secretly find this stereotype rather flattering. But their blood freezes when "smart" is a euphemism for "cunning" or "sneaky;" or if "successful" infers "trying to take over the world and enslave everybody" or "rich" implies "greedy blood-suckers."

But is the basic *positive* stereotype true?

Social theorist Dr. Charles Murray discovered that, on average, Ashkenazic Jews have an IQ (whatever IQ tests are worth) of 7-15 points higher than average. Furthermore, Jews represent less than 2% of the US population, yet comprise around 37% of American

Nobel prize winners, 14% of doctors, and 15% of scientists.

Median American Jewish income stands at $54,000 a year (this is down from $80,000 prior to the 21st century recession) and 34% of American Jewish households report an income of over $75,000 a year.

91% of American Jews finish high school and 65% finish college.

However, poor Jews definitely exist and Jewish communities throughout the world find it necessary to provide food drives, Sabbath provisions, and financial assistance for their fellow Jews.

The Jewish population also suffers from learning disabilities, autism, PDD, Down's syndrome, or just plain lack of skill in some area—just like everyone else.

Jews of average to poor economic status do feel the differences when among other Jews who generally fare better financially. This is not intentional, but occurs naturally when one lives in a less prestigious neighborhood, wears generic brand clothing, goes on cheap vacations, and sends one's children to a regular public school rather than a private school or an upscale public school.

Jewish children from families who can't afford the finer things in life keenly feel the differences in a Jewish camp or Hebrew school when surrounded by peers who vacation in Hawaii or the Bahamas, attend private school, wear designer clothing, live in upscale homes, and whose parents who hold prestigious jobs. Again, even if the wealthier peers are in no way snobbish about their lifestyle, the differences are starkly felt.

In fact, the public school I attended during junior high served students from mostly lower economic neighborhoods. Yet in the evenings, I attended Hebrew school in an upscale area. This meant that I spent my days in a place where I had to dress down and drop my g's ("nothin' " instead of "nothing") or maybe get bullied. Some students could only afford second-hand clothing and some were either too poor or too neglected to even receive eyeglasses. One classmate regularly came to school drunk by 8 AM. Then I spent a couple of evenings a week at Hebrew school where I was the only one who returned from winter break without a ski tag dangling from my coat zipper, who didn't know how "Esprit" was pronounced, and who had never heard of Guess jeans, let alone worn them. (Sorry about all the Eighties references.) But I gained a lot from shuttling between the different worlds and the experiences were good for me. And they provide my children with funny stories like the following:

I invited one of my classmates (we'll call her Melanie) to my bat mitzvah and the next day, she approached me, her eyes shining, and said, "I can come, but my aunt says that I need a fur coat 'cause all Jews have fur coats and I can't come to a Jewish church without one."

"Um, it's called a synagogue," I said.

She gave me a bewildered smile. "Okay."

Quite used to this kind of misunderstanding, I just replied, "Right, um, just so you know? It's not a Jewish church, it's called a synagogue. They're completely different."

With the same smile, she shrugged her shoulders and said, "Whatever."

Then I frowned in puzzlement and said, "It can't be true about the fur coats because I've never seen anyone there in a fur coat." I frowned again. "I think people don't wear fur coats because they feel it's not ethical to kill an animal just for its fur." (Remember: Non-Orthodox Jews, which is what I was, grow up in passionately liberal environments.)

Melanie kind of laughed and said, "Well—fur coats. That's what my aunt said." Her eyes lit up even more.

"She can call my mom, if she wants," I said. "My mom will tell her."

Melanie looked alarmed. "No," she said. "My aunt *knows*!"

I realized that Melanie really wanted that fur coat.

And she showed up to my bat mitzvah in a fur coat bought specially for the occasion by her well-meaning aunt—the only fur coat there—and didn't take it off the whole time.

Going on to the next stage of life, Jews who never attended college or are college drop-outs may also feel mildly awkward when surrounded by their degreed peers. For example, "What did you major in?" is a typical question in the Jewish community and being the only who answers, "I didn't" or "I majored in liberal arts, but never finished my degree" can be uncomfortable, even if the questioner isn't remotely condescending about it.

In the ultra-Orthodox community, only 25% of ultra-Orthodox Jews finish college, although many of those who don't go to college still receive some kind of higher education, like a two-year degree in graphic design or business. In contrast, 65% of Modern Orthodox Jews graduate from college.

The whole topic of Jewish success is uncomfortable for Jews outside of their own circles because bigots possess a "damned if you do/damned if you don't" attitude. When faced with accusations of being parasites or leeches, Jews emphasize their contributions to society. Yet when Jews are accused of dominating the world, they'll downplay their role and point to the poverty level (particularly in Israel) or to the Holocaust, the Inquisition, and the many acts of discrimination and genocides against Jews throughout history.

Jews are Stingy

Not more than anybody else! In fact, Jews give tons of charity (called *tzedakah*) and Jewish law obligates Jews to give a minimum of 10% of their income to charity. The 2012 National Study of Jewish American Giving revealed that 76% of non-Orthodox American Jews made a charitable contribution that year, the median being $1200. (In comparison, 63% of non-Jews donated a median of $600 that same year.) The big shocker was that Jews gave a lot more to non-Jewish causes than to Jewish ones. In fact, 21% of Jews contributed exclusively to non-Jewish causes.

(Interestingly, the study excluded Orthodox Jews because "their substantially higher degree of religious engagement, compared to non-Orthodox Jews, skews data." What does that even mean? I'm not completely sure, but in following Torah law, Orthodox Jews tend to give more *tzedakah* and being of the "Clean-Up-Your-Own-Backyard-First" variety, they primarily give to Jewish organizations and the Jewish poor—although they also contribute to general disaster relief collections and the like. I guess that's the skewer.)

This stereotype of stinginess seems to have its roots in the Middle Ages when Jews were forced to work as money-lenders and innkeepers due to European ordinances against letting Jews own land or join guilds. Booze-guzzling peasants wanted to run up tabs they could never pay off. And money-lenders had to take interest in order to feed their families and pay a percentage to the rulers, although Jewish money-lenders lent at lower interest rates than Christian money-lenders, according to Barbara Tuchman's *A Distant Mirror: The Calamitous Fourteenth Century*.

Jews aren't Athletic

This stereotype has no real foundation. American Jewish boys have always played baseball, though they have turned to basketball in more recent generations. Likely, this stereotype developed from the low Jewish representation in *professional* sports. That, and many Jewish writers haven't been so athletic and project themselves onto the Jewish characters they create for books and movies.

So while professional Jewish success leans toward the cerebral or social arenas, there have still been several Jewish Olympians and professional players.

Jewish teenagers often join sports teams. Basketball is hugely popular among Jewish boys, including Orthodox boys. Jewish boys are also often found on track, crew, and swim teams, and even in wrestling and football. Jewish girls often join the female sports teams, which also include cheerleading and gymnastics. But it's true that Jews do not usually continue on to the professional level of sports. Yet some do.

Are Jews as Materialistic, Opinionated, Loud, Pushy, and Neurotic as Portrayed by Jewish Comedians?

Whaddaya mean?!

No. In fact, this stereotype represents a minority. There are many refined, quiet, thoughtful, gracious Jews.

However, it does seem like Jews tend to be more emotionally expressive than non-Jews. Or maybe just the ones from New York (where most American Jews live) because New Yorkers themselves are pretty forthright about their attitudes. On the other hand, this also seems to be generational and the longer Jews are in America, the less "Jewish" they act in contrast to the surrounding culture.

Jews don't usually feel neurotic or overly self-conscious about their Judaism; in fact, they often feel positively about it.

And many of the Jews who are loud and opinionated also possess hearts of gold and are loyal people who can always be called upon for any favor.

What about Jewish Mothers?

Like any caring mother—Jewish or not—many Jewish mothers (and fathers) tend to be very involved with their children's lives. But not all of them are. And most aren't neurotic or pushy or materialistic about it. Unfortunately, those Jewish mothers who were neurotic or pushy or materialistic seemed to have produced more than their share of writers and comedians.

Jews Talk Funny

There is a Jewish-American accent. (There is also a Jewish-British accent.) It's similar to the New York accents. You'll hear it in New York and among many Orthodox Jews, even if they don't live in New York. The Jewish accent is most pronounced among Yiddish-speaking communities. Among many Hassidic Jews, there is often a slight European lilt to their Jewish-New York accent. At the same time, an Orthodox Jew born and raised in, say, Seattle will speak with the same accent as any other Seattleite. Charleston Jews have a Southern accent. And so on.

Many Jews outside of the Orthodox community and outside of the large Jewish hubs don't really relate to the stereotypical speech popular in Jewish comedy. They can even be embarrassed by it.

Jews and Names

Are All Jews Named Rachel or Deborah or Rebecca— or Josh or David or Adam?

No. In fact, most aren't.

Okay, there are a lot of Jewish Joshes and Davids. More than there are Jewish Rachels and Deborahs and Leahs.

But most Jews outside the Orthodox community name their children regular American names. In the Eighties, I felt like all the Jewish girls were named Melissa, Jessica, Lisa, and Stacey. In the Nineties, they all seemed to be called Jen. There were a lot of Jewish boys named Josh, David, and Michael, but the rest seemed to be called Mark or Jeff.

Today, Jewish girls are often called Emma, Maddie, or Nora, while Jewish boys are often called Jack, Ethan, or Collin. Or anything else their parents like.

Do All Jews whose Last Names aren't Cohen or Levi have Last Names that End in either "berg" or "stein" or "man"?

Many do, of course. But many Jews do not have identifiably Jewish last names. Lots of Jews—including

Orthodox Jews—possess last names like Miller, Brown, Nelson, and Robinson.

Non-Jewish children born to Jewish fathers can have stereotypical Jewish surnames like "Goldberg" or "Katz."

Converts to Judaism or Jewish children with non-Jewish fathers can even have last names like Christensen or Huang. (Okay, if an Orthodox convert possesses an obviously Christian name, he often changes it.)

Sefardic Jews often have last names that reflect their Arabic or Spanish heritage, like Alhadef, Dweck, Pinto, or Calvo.

What about Hebrew Names?

Many Jews do not give their child a Hebrew name. But many Jews do. The child may never use it, depending. Some teachers at Jewish schools use their students' Hebrew names, even if the child normally goes by an English name. Sometimes parents choose the Hebrew version of the English name, like Jonathan as the Anglicized version of Yonatan. In other cases, they want to name the child after a deceased relative, so they'll give the child an English name that starts with the same letter as the deceased's Hebrew name, regardless of whether that is the Hebrew version of the English name. For example, Aharon is the original Hebrew name of Aaron. But if the parents want to name their son after Uncle Al, whose Hebrew name was Avraham, then Aaron's Hebrew name will be Avraham. Sound complicated? But it's really common among those who choose to give their child a Hebrew name.

Orthodox Jews always have a Hebrew or Yiddish name, but they might have an English name that they use, especially in business where they might feel that it's easier for non-Jewish people to use the name "Jerry" as opposed to "Yeḥezkel" (Ezekiel).

What is Hebrew School?

Hebrew school is a Jewish studies school that takes place outside of regular school hours. It serves Jewish students who attend non-Jewish public or private schools. Each session is around 2 hours long. Sometimes it's open just on Sundays (and called Sunday school). It can start in kindergarten and run through 12th grade. Sometimes it's once or twice a week in the afternoon/evening. Usually, the Hebrew alphabet is taught along with some very basic Hebrew grammar and vocabulary, but many students come out of it unable to read Hebrew and even those who learn to read Hebrew may understand virtually nothing, depending on the school. Hebrew prayer and Jewish history are also included. For older students, Hebrew school may offer a wide range of topics from Jewish scholarship to Jewish current events to Jewish politics to Jewish cooking. The amount and variety depends on each community's resources.

What Goes on in Jewish Youth Groups?

First of all, there are interdenominational groups like Bnai Brith Youth Organization and Young Judea. Then there are the Conservative USY (United Synagogue Youth), the Reform NFTY (National Federation of Temple Youth), and the Modern Orthodox NCSY (National Conference of Synagogue Youth). They may offer weekly meetings, weekend retreats, regional conferences, national conferences, and international conferences (which often aren't so international; it mostly means that Americans and Canadians get together). They normally include community service and volunteer work. These organizations can also run Jewish summer camps.

Originally, Jewish parents encouraged their children to join these organizations as a way to make Jewish friends and eventually marry fellow Jews—and this is still true among the Orthodox organizations. However, with the high rate of intermarriage and non-kosher conversions outside of the Orthodox community, many of the Jewish youth group participants today aren't actually Jewish (although they may genuinely think they are).

Ultra-Orthodox communities don't organize national youth groups, but arrange local alternatives, such as afterschool clubs, summer camps, volunteer programs, and Sabbath activities.

What's Yiddish?

"Yiddish" literally means "Jewish." Formally known as Judeo-German, it is a German-based language that developed among the Jewish communities of Europe. It is mostly a blend of Jewish-accented German and Ashkenazic-accented Hebrew with some Aramaic (a Semitic language of ancient Babylonia) and a sprinkling of words from other European languages. It is traditionally written with Hebrew letters. Different regions developed different Yiddish pronunciations and incorporated bits of the local language into their regional Yiddish. For example, Russian Yiddish contains lots of Russian. I remember one elderly Jewish immigrant who joked, "I know six languages—Russian Yiddish, German Yiddish, Polish Yiddish, Hungarian Yiddish, Hebrew, and English."

The Yiddish slang familiar to Americans was introduced through the entertainment industry by secular Yiddish-speaking Jewish immigrants. Most of the uncomplimentary Yiddish words Americans routinely use in place of "jerk" are actually extremely vulgar in origin and should not be used with people who actually know Yiddish.

Most people aren't aware of the worldwide development of Jewish languages based on local languages. After Yiddish, the far second is Judeo-Spanish—Ladino. Sefardic communities from the Mediterranean still incorporate Ladino into their daily conversations and prayers. There are also dialects of Judeo-Arabic and Judeo-Farsi, but these are quickly dying out. The Ladino song, *El Rey Nimrod*, remains a popular vestige of Ladino, but only Yiddish remains in wide use, spoken exclusively in some communities, with some Orthodox schools in America, England, and Israel conducting all classes in Yiddish. (Yes, they learn math and geography in Yiddish.) When non-Orthodox Jews start interacting with the ultra-Orthodox community, they are often surprised to discover that Yiddish is nowhere near the "dead" language they'd always been told it was.

Is "Goy" a Slur?

No. *Goy* is Hebrew for "nation." The plural of *goy* is *goyim*. In ancient liturgy, the Jewish nation is referred to as a *goy kadosh*—a holy nation. The famous Biblical verse "One nation shall not lift a sword against another nation" uses the word *goy*. Jewish scholarly works traditionally use words synonymous with "nations" to refer to non-Jews and refer to a righteous gentile by the same word used to refer to a righteous Jew: *tzaddik*—the full term is "the righteous ones of the nations" (meaning the righteous gentiles). In fact, *goy* is not the most common term used.

So why did *goy* became popular? Probably because that was the word of choice in Yiddish.

CHAPTER SIX

Jews and Non-Jews

General Jewish Attitude toward Non-Jews

For Jews living in Western culture, things have never been so good (although in recent years, acts of bigotry against Jews have increased). Jewish immigrants have always felt grateful for the freedoms they experienced in America and their descendants have embraced and contributed to American society wholeheartedly.

Many Jews even feel more American than they feel Jewish. Many Jews don't want to stand out as "Jewish," even if they feel positive about their Jewish identity. They feel perfectly comfortable with looking, dressing, and acting like any other American, and they feel truly bonded with their non-Jewish friends and relatives.

The Intrinsic Attitude of Judaism toward Non-Jews

Judaism itself regards every human being as having been made in God's image, as stated at the beginning of Genesis.

Proselytism of non-Jews is strictly forbidden by Judaism because Judaism recognizes that one need not be Jewish to "get into Heaven." In fact, if you're not Jewish, you can earn a lovely Eternity merely by upholding following laws:

1) *Don't worship anyone but God (including no praying to a "son" of God; anyway, Judaism considers God as having many sons and daughters, not just one; furthermore, while a human being can be holy, he or she can never be God)*

2) *Don't steal (this includes severe prohibitions against kidnapping and rape)*

3) *Don't murder (includes suicide & most abortions)*

4) *Establish courts of true justice (and if your government or society doesn't let you, then at least support true justice in your heart and in all your actions as much as you can)*

5) *Don't tear a limb from a living animal*

6) *Don't engage in any kind of sexual immorality (this includes same-gender marriage)*

7) *Don't curse God*

These are also known as the Seven Noahide Commandments (or the Seven Laws of Noah) because they are mentioned in the story of Noah, who was not Jewish, yet is described as having "walked with God" and himself observed these Seven Laws. They are considered the standard to which every non-Jew should strive.

For more details, please go to:

www.simpletoremember.com/articles/a/seven-laws-of-noah/

In the Talmud, the Sages use the example of a non-Jewish Roman council president named Dama ben Netina as a prime example of how one should honor one's parents. The stories of Dama ben Netina are well-known throughout the Orthodox world and Orthodox Jews learn about him from a young age.

Judaism believes that every person, Jew or not, will receive his or her portion in the World to Come according to his or her deeds. For example, a Jew who murders and lies and cheats will theoretically find himself in Hell while a non-Jew who behaves with justice, morality, and compassion will find himself in Heaven. Okay, that is a wild oversimplification, but you get the general idea.

Anti-Jewish Bigotry

Jews sometimes get attacked or even killed for being Jewish. Males wearing a *kippah* (and thus identifiably Jewish) are at the greatest risk for this, which is why many American Orthodox parents send their boys to self-defense classes.

Here's a true story I heard from the boy himself:

A secular Jewish boy was sitting in a forest after his bar mitzvah, seriously contemplating whether he should start wearing a *kippah* all the time. He wasn't at all religious, but he felt a certain something and thought maybe wearing a *kippah* was the best way to express that "something." He placed the *kippah* on his head and sat there, getting the feel of it, when a group of neo-Nazi skinheads saw him and attacked. Fortunately, he lived through it. Later, determined that a lack of physical prowess would never prevent him from expressing his religious feelings again, he joined a kick-boxing class and eventually became a national kick-boxing champion. Later, he immigrated to Israel where he wore his *kippah* as much as he darn wanted.

In another instance, a cute, bubbly Jewish girl I knew was grabbed by a classmate who pressed a knife against her throat and snarled, "[Bleep] you, you Jewish [bleep]!"

At some point, Jews are called names or verbally abused for being Jewish. This can happen at school or on the street. Or a "friend" might start tossing coins at her Jewish classmate as a "joke." During the time when history class covers World War II, a hand-written sign may appear upon the classroom door which says, *JEWS! GO BACK TO AUSCHWITZ!*

A teacher told me in the middle of history class that we Jews had invented the Holocaust and smirked as I argued with him. The rest of the class just sat there, bored. (And no, I didn't report him. I told my parents, who then praised me for my well-reasoned arguments against him, and that was as far as it went.)

Despite feeling cut deep when encountering bigotry, Jewish students usually do not talk about it (except maybe to their friends or if it comes up as topic of discussion at a Jewish youth group meeting or convention) and often don't tell their parents or teachers, unless it's ongoing or severe. (Orthodox Jews tend to be more open to talking about and take it less to heart, unless it's severe.) Actually, the first time it happens, Jewish kids do tell their parents, who usually tell them to just ignore it. Teachers rarely do anything useful and Jews learn early on that they are basically on their own when faced with bigotry, although they can usually count on one or two non-Jewish friends rising to their defense. Because Jewish kids quickly learn that anti-Jewish bigotry doesn't really prevent them from accomplishing their goals and dreams, they generally try to ignore it. If things get violent and there are enough enthusiastic Jewish boys, they may form a gang which targets only those who harmed them. However, most Jewish kids find each event shocking because they feel so much a part of American society, and find prejudice so personally abhorrent, they genuinely can't understand why bigots feel the way they do.

At work, bigoted co-workers and bosses tend to be much more subtle. The bigotry comes out through tight smirks and little comments. Some don't outright say or do anything, but seem clearly uncomfortable around Jews. Unless the bigot actively obstructs the Jew in his or her career or goals, or becomes abusive, the Jewish colleague usually works around the situation.

To head off antagonism before it starts, many Jews try to overcompensate. For example, Jews who want to leave early on Fridays in order to get home in time for winter Sabbaths (when the sun sets in the afternoon) will usually work later on other days or come in on Sundays. Jews who never work on Saturdays will also work more hours on other days to compensate. In fact, many Jews set up an informal arrangement with a Christian co-worker in which the Christian co-worker agrees to cover the Jewish co-worker on Saturdays and the Jew agrees to cover the Christian on Sundays, which works out to their mutual benefit. Jewish employers who close their offices for Jewish holidays often give their non-Jewish employees a bonus to cover those non-working days.

Because diversity and tolerance are such a huge part of their self-image, the secular liberals who don't like Jews (as opposed to the secular liberals who are truly open-minded) try to disguise it—even from themselves. Many knowledgeable Jews consider the growing anti-Israel sentiment, especially popular in mainstream media and on college campuses, to be a politically correct form of Jew-hatred.

Totally assimilated Jews in secular liberal communities occasionally deal with comments like, "Omigosh, she really needs a professional to do something about that Jewish hair!" Or, "I was really

Jewed down." Usually, the Jew in the room says something like, "Um, Morgan—I'm Jewish...." Or a friend says, "Uh, Morgan...did you know that Emma is Jewish?" An uncomfortable silence usually follows and then "Morgan" either shrugs or mutters "Sorry" and changes the subjects.

In general, Jews deal with anti-Jewish bigotry by ignoring it, attempting to educate it, or taking it to court. If things get violent, the Jew can react in kind, but only if he or she feels skilled enough to do so. For example, a young man once exposed himself to a Ḥassidic friend of mine as she accidentally walked through the Muslim Quarter of the Old City of Jerusalem. She pointed and laughed, then continued walking. He attacked her from behind, not knowing that she was well-trained in self-defense. She flipped him over and beat him up, then went to the police.

Jews and Christians

Some Christians feel very fond of Jews, have no desire to convert them, and are staunch supporters of Jewish rights, especially in Israel. Likewise, some are fascinated by Jews and are very excited to meet one. Some relate to Jews normally—just as they do to everyone else. Some are very uncomfortable around Jews. And some despise Jews.

And the exact same can also be said of non-Christians.

Yet the proselytizing factor within Christianity—however well-intentioned—is quite prominent and problematic for Jews. The bottom line is that the idea of accepting a human being as God or worshiped as a god is completely forbidden by Judaism—as dictated by God Himself. And even as a regular human being, Jesus didn't fit the requirements for the Messiah as specified by Judaism. Yet some Christians very earnestly want to convert their Jewish friends, neighbors, co-workers, and classmates, and Jews usually find them annoying, even if they appreciate their misguided sincerity and good character.

However, Jews find actual missionaries to be very disturbing. Jews realize that many Christian missionaries target Jews, going out of their way to specifically debate Jews or knock on the doors of Jewish homes, as if converting a Jew is a bigger notch in their belt. Jews generally deal with these types in a polite yet firm manner, but can get really upset if the proselytizing is unrelenting and rude or targets Jewish children, or is just plain creepy as with the missionary organizations that stoop to using highly sophisticated deception and manipulation to target Jews, methods which even incorporate the latest technology.

Most Jews don't actually mind the Christmas and Easter decorations and music popular during those seasons. (However, the inundation of it bothers them about as much as it bothers everyone else.) Many secular Jews know several Christmas carols by heart and enjoy the friendly atmosphere and parties.

But most Jews firmly support the separation of Church and State because of the frightening history of European Christian persecution against Jews. Secular liberal American Jews sometimes take this separation to an unnecessary extreme. But proselytizing, aggressive and deceptive missionaries, Christian bigots, and the anti-Jewish sentiment in some American churches keep this wariness alive in many American Jews. While the vast majority of American Christians find the idea of pogroms, religious coercion (such as kidnapping, brainwashing, and torture), hate-filled rhetoric, and discrimination of any kind absolutely repugnant, history (particularly in Europe) has left its imprint on the Jewish psyche. This, despite there being much more dangerous threats to Jews than Christianity in the public schools—or the clear fact that, until the move toward secularism over the past decades, Jews lived safely and happily in what America once was—a country with a strong Christian character. Unfortunately, this wariness has led some well-meaning yet misguided Jews to support the separation of God and State (even by Jews who themselves believe in God) when in actuality, the Christian-backed proposals for non-religion-specific practices—such as a moment of silence for personal prayer in the public schools or the Ten Commandments in a court house—are much more in line with core Jewish values than the current drift toward complete secularism.

Another misunderstanding occurs because Judaism is defined by birth (or rigorous conversion), and not by belief (as it is in Christianity). So secular Jews sometimes end up referring to any non-Jew as "Christian," even if that person isn't Christian at all.

CHAPTER SEVEN

Orthodox Jews

M any Americans, including Jews themselves, go through their whole life without ever meeting an Orthodox Jew. In contrast, many people know several Jews who are Conservative or Reform or "just plain Jewish."

People tend to know the least about Orthodox Jews.

Frankly, I don't recall ever having seen an accurate portrayal of Orthodox Jews in books or movies—even among those written by Orthodox Jews. (Then again, I have not seen every single movie or book featuring Orthodox Jews.) For example, *Ushpizin* is one of the best movies I've ever seen. Using superior acting skills, a well-written script, and outstanding humor, *Ushpizin* conveys core Jewish concepts and rituals— and these are shown accurately. But is it representative of the Jewish people of Israel? At best, the characters are appealing caricatures.

Even non-fiction avenues, like journalism, mess up. And even when the portrayal is positive, it is still usually not accurate. The complexity and diversity within the Orthodox community make it very easy to produce basic, obvious mistakes. And that's aside from all the artistic license filmmakers and writers naturally take.

Furthermore, even Orthodox Jews don't always know all the nitty-gritty details of what other Orthodox groups do, though they do have a basic idea. Even among Ḥassidic Jews, one Ḥassidic group is not necessarily familiar with all the customs of another Ḥassidic group.

Furthermore, one Orthodox Jew's experience within one community is exactly that: one person's experience. That person may experience the community in a vastly different way than, say, 80% of everybody else in that community. That specific experience may be true, but not representative—even if that person portrays it as representative.

So Orthodox Jews end up seeing mistakes and misrepresentations that their 4-year-old nephew could catch. (And then Orthodox Jews are bombarded with the well-meaning, good-natured question: "Do you guys *really* do that?" And they have to say no. And then they have to explain why. And then they are asked to explain why, if it's not true, did the book or movie portray things that way? And so on. It's not offensive or anything, it's just pointless.)

So despite its stereotype of being a homogeneous, closed, narrow-minded society, the Orthodox community is actually quite complex and diverse.

A Basic Misunderstanding of Orthodox Jews

One of the hardest things to understand about Orthodox Jews (and one of the biggest frustrations for Orthodox Jews when dealing with Jews who aren't Orthodox or with people who aren't Jewish) is the emphasis Judaism places on authenticity and inner motivation. All commandments, for example, are meant to be carried out with wholehearted sincerity and joy—or at the very least, with as much wholehearted sincerity and joy as one can muster up at any given moment. For example, Orthodox Jews are well-aware of religious hypocrisy or weak commitment and the like, and will consider such people "not so *frum*" regardless of how they're dressed and what synagogue they attend.

Along these same lines, certificates and other formalities (like synagogue membership, conversion certificates, and rabbinical ordination) don't mean to Orthodox Jews what they mean to those outside of Orthodox Judaism. For example, Orthodox Jews know that rabbinical ordination only means that the rabbi passed a strenuous test of scholarship. And many tests of rabbinical ordination are limited to one area of Jewish law—a large area, to be sure, but not all-encompassing. And it says nothing about one's character or ability to apply the laws with wisdom. Through rigorous learning, one may acquire all one needs to know without ever obtaining official rabbinic certification, although if, say, rabbinical ordination from an institution known for rigorous testing of a wide breadth of Jewish law and also for the examiners knowledge of the subject's personal integrity, then that ordination will be taken very seriously. But as it goes, one may be called "Rabbi" simply on the basis of his knowledge alone, whether he received official ordination or not.

So why even bother getting official ordination? Well, it's evidence of the acquirement of a certain amount of knowledge and some places insist on it as hiring prerequisite.

As mentioned earlier, Orthodox Jews don't even use the word Orthodox among themselves. They use the Yiddish word *frum*, which basically means "religious" and is much more accurate and meaningful than the awkward term "Orthodox."

This dynamic shows up in conversations like this:

Challenger: "Orthodox Jews are such hypocrites. I know this Orthodox guy and I always see him eating hot dogs from the non-kosher stand."

Orthodox Jew: "Um, well, then that means he's not so Orthodox." (Meanwhile, he's thinking: *Boy, I wish I could say "frum"!*)

Challenger: "But he belongs to an Orthodox synagogue! And he wears that beanie-thing!"

Orthodox Jew: "Well, a lot of people belong to Orthodox synagogues, but aren't actually Orthodox. It's the same with guys like him who wear a *kippah*—I mean, that beanie-thing." (Meanwhile, the Orthodox Jew is thinking, *Okay, so the guy isn't so frum. He wears a kippah and goes to a frum shul [Orthodox synagogue], but he's actually not so frum. What's the big deal? And I hate saying "Orthodox." That's part of what's making this so hard to explain....)*

Challenger: "How can you belong to an Orthodox synagogue and not be Orthodox?"

Orthodox Jew: "Because you just can. Maybe he just likes it. Anyway, everyone is at their own level and doing their individual religious best. Everyone is strong in one religious area and weak in another. But really, that guy isn't so Orthodox."

Challenger: "But I *saw....*"

And so on.

As mentioned, even with conversions, an Orthodox conversion certificate means little to Orthodox Jews if it's clear that the convert was not sincere. In fact, Orthodox rabbis who perform conversions for improper motives (like for money or because the potential convert wants to marry a Jew), or without checking the potential convert's sincerity, eventually find that their conversions are not accepted by Orthodox institutions, communities, and schools.

I remember a woman who "converted" to Judaism, mostly to rattle her parents, but also to have something extra in common with her Jewish fiancé. She managed to find an old depressed Orthodox rabbi who headed an increasingly assimilating congregation, and who resigned himself to performing the "conversion" and giving her a certificate. Meanwhile, she continued to fry up cheeseburgers at home and keep basically nothing of Torah law—although she did light Ḥanukah candles every year and at first, regularly attended Sabbath services at that rabbi's synagogue, always arriving by car despite this being a clear violation of Jewish Sabbath law (although she later switched to a Reform synagogue and dropped synagogue attendance altogether). Of course, she boasted of having proof of an "Orthodox" conversion. She was perturbed that Orthodox Jews would not recognize her conversion and could not accept that her proclaimed observance of Judaism was in complete violation of actual Jewish law and belief.

In summary, Judaism places prime importance on a person's actual actions and inner motivations. This is an integral part of Judaism. (Remember, the whole idea of categorizing Jews into different religious groups was invented by Jews who rejected Judaism.) For example, according to basic Judaism, a secular Jew who is trying to become more religious is on a higher spiritual level than a seemingly Orthodox Jew who apathetically observes Jewish law by rote and is looking to be more secular. Spiritually speaking, that secular Jew is moving up and that seemingly Orthodox Jew is moving down. Yet by outside appearances, it looks the opposite. But God knows what's really going on. Many Orthodox Jews are raised with this awareness. It actually allows for a lot of flexibility and individuality, but is hard to explain to others.

Orthodox Stereotype Busters

The Big, Big Misconception: Do Orthodox Jews have Their Spouses Chosen for Them?

Pretty much false.

Orthodox Jews often get set up on dates via a matchmaker. It's very similar to going out on a blind date, except with more pre-date research. At some point, the time comes to search for a spouse—commonly called *basheret* (Divinely ordained) in Yiddish or *zivug* (Divinely ordained marital partner) in Hebrew. Sometimes, the child brings it up with the parents first. Often, the parents bring it up first. In some communities, there is a set age at which people start looking. Sometimes, someone else—like a relative, neighbor, or friend—suggests someone who seems compatible with the Orthodox single. People often turn to an official matchmaker (called a *shadḥan*). Then there is a vetting process in which names and information are presented and recommendations given. The parents contact neighbors, teachers, friends, former roommates, co-workers, and anyone else with insight into the character of the suggested match. If the unmarried person is already an independent adult, such as a formerly secular Jew who became Orthodox on his or her own, or someone divorced or widowed, they will often manage the vetting process themselves while utilizing the assistance of friends and relatives. Many consult with their personal rabbi and/or rebbetzin for guidance. And despite the stereotype of the professional matchmaker as a not-completely-honest busybody who just wants to see everyone married off at all costs, most take their job very seriously and make good consultants because they truly want to see people settle down with a compatible spouse.

Because a spouse can either make or break one's life, the search is taken very seriously. There is a serious push to unearth any possible genetic diseases, mental illness, character issues, or just plain incompatibilities that could cause problems during the marriage.

After the parents (or searching single) determine that the suggested man or woman is a potentially good match, they set up a date.

Because Modern Orthodoxy includes such a vast range of practice, from the nearly ultra-Orthodox to the nearly secular, the dating process may either be very similar to the above, or singles may meet as they do in the secular world and date with no intention of marriage. Many Modern Orthodox married couples meet through youth groups, work, or synagogue, and don't use a matchmaker or vetting process at all. (But the dating process itself is done with the intent of determining marital compatibility.)

How and where this happens depends on the community. For many, the guy shows up at the girl's home, meets the parents, then drives the girl out to a hotel lobby or cafe or restaurant for non-alcoholic drinks. Or they may go to a park or garden or promenade. Sometimes, they meet at someone's home. Or else they arrange to arrive separately at one of these places. This first meeting usually lasts for 2-4 hours. The couple continues to meet either until one decides the other is not for him/her or they mutually agree to marry. This is usually done within 10 dates or less.

In certain Ḥassidic communities, the investigative work is done so thoroughly that all that is left is for the couple to decide if they like each other. (In such a community, only one meeting is required.) The match is also run past the Rebbe for approval. The guy is brought to the girl's house (or the house of her aunt or grandmother) and then they are sent for a walk or out to the porch or yard, or the parents leave them in the living room and go "hide" in one of the bedrooms or in the kitchen. Inquisitive younger siblings are made scarce for such occasions. Sometimes, the outcome is so certain that while the couple meets, the parents are in another room working out the details of the wedding and living expenses.

Very rarely, the match is decided (likely by the Rebbe) before the couple even meets. But they still meet at some point before the wedding just to be sure.

Jewish law forbids a marriage from taking place without the agreement of both partners. This law is derived from the biblical story of Rebecca and Isaac, in which Rebecca's family insisted on asking Rebecca whether she wanted to go marry Isaac, and only consented to the match when Rebecca gave her own consent.

In the olden days, due to distances and cultural norms, the couple often did not meet before the wedding. So the precept of seeing each other was fulfilled either by pointing out the intended among a crowd or when the groom came to place the veil on the bride right before the actual ceremony. And while you might think that must have been tricky—after all, who would reject their intended at the wedding?—

there is a well-known story from 100 years ago of a Jerusalem groom who decided during the wedding that he just couldn't go through with it. She was a nice girl, but he simply found her so unattractive, he realized he just couldn't do it. Fortunately, his roommate—who had heard all about her fine qualities from discussions with the groom in an effort to convince himself that her inner beauty overrode her outer appearance—literally stepped up to the plate to save her from embarrassment and asked her to marry him. She agreed and the wedding ceremony continued with the roommate as the groom and they lived happily ever after. Really.

Occasionally, an unmarried person may feel pressured into a match or feel that they shouldn't reject it because how could they know better than their wise parents? But he or she always has the Torah-mandated right to refuse for any reason and can get rabbinical backing for that refusal.

What many people don't realize is that love at first sight can happen even in these situations. The couple meets and is immediately zapped by mutual chemistry. This can happen even in the above-mentioned Ḥassidic communities. People also fall in love after their wedding. Some couples never fall romantically in love, so to speak, but enjoy a lifelong relationship of friendship and camaraderie. And alas, some never get along. Divorce is permitted in Judaism, and while divorce is rising in the Orthodox community, it is not common and considered a very last resort.

Do Ḥassidic Jews Worship Their Rebbe?

Children and teenagers aside, most Ḥassidic Jews don't worship their Rebbe, but they do hold him in high esteem. Once upon a time, a Ḥassidic Rebbe (pronounced REH-bee or REH-beh) was a man of lofty spiritual stature. They were truly holy, possessed amazing vision and foresight, and many were miracle-workers. One of the last Rebbes to be seen this way was the last Lubavitcher Rebbe, who passed away in 1994 (and has not been replaced, nor is there any intention to inaugurate a new Rebbe in his place).

Today, most Ḥassids consider their Rebbes to be highly intelligent and dedicated people of great skill and caring. And they are loyal in the way that people are to a leader who has dedicated his life to them and in the way that people are to their family traditions. Just like you have people who say, "In my family, we all play softball." "We only vote Democrat." "We only attend Harvard." "We only root for the Yankees."

Sure, there are people—just like anywhere in the world—who can get wound up out of a warped sense of loyalty, which may have little to do with the reality. Try insulting the team of a hot-headed sports fans, even if he himself knows it's true that his team hasn't won a game in decades or that his favorite player is jerk who could also be doing a lot better in the game. But it's his team, darn it, and you'd better not start up.

How much influence the Rebbe has over someone's life has more to do with the individual Ḥassid than with the Rebbe, although the group's dynamic also plays a part. One Ḥassid may consult with the Rebbe only for something major, like complicated surgery and the like. Another may consult with the Rebbe regularly for both minor and major decisions. Some Rebbes provide specific strictures and customs that cover significant details of his followers' lives. Other Rebbes offer a less structured framework.

Many Rebbes also earn the love and respect of those outside their immediate group. It is not uncommon for a Jew belonging to another group to consult with another Rebbe or donate to that Rebbe's group. Completely secular Jews and non-Jews sometimes also seek out a relationship with a Rebbe who impresses them as approachable and wise.

Whether the Rebbe is actually a saintly man of true holiness and far-seeing vision or "merely" a tireless, multi-tasking genius (as many are today), the Rebbe is a point of unification and provides highly valued structure and guidance.

Non-Ḥassidic Ashkenazic (*Litvak*), Sefardic, and Modern Orthodox Jews usually also have a spiritual leader, to whom they refer to by the Hebrew word "Rav" (Rabbi) and can develop the same relationship and attitude toward him that a Ḥassid does with his Rebbe. And, like the Rebbe, sometimes a Rav is sought out by secular Jews or non-Jews.

For the benefit of their followers, both a Rebbe and a Rav may keep tabs on who is the best doctor for specific situations, the location of good real estate and good schools, good therapists, and so on.

Their supporters benefit from these practical recommendations and also from their personal advice

Many Orthodox women, in addition to a Rebbe or Rav, also have a Rebbetzin (Yiddish) or Rabbanit (Hebrew: rabba-NEET) to whom they go for guidance. This relationship is far less formal than the one with a Rebbe or Rav and is similar to that of a mentor or a beloved aunt.

Orthodox Jews and Non-Orthodox Jews

In general, Orthodox Jews across the board feel a strong affinity for their fellow Jews—including the most assimilated Jews—and this affinity often even extends toward secular Jews who look down on Orthodox Jews. (Orthodox Jews generally understand that such a person either underwent a negative experience or suffers from misconceptions propagated by the mainstream media or by their non-Orthodox synagogues and institutions.) Like most Jews regardless of background, Orthodox Jews feel responsible toward fellow Jews throughout the world and often go out of their way to make non-Orthodox Jews feel comfortable around them. (Some do this more gracefully then others.) Even regarding now-secular Jews who were born into Orthodox families and attended Orthodox schools, Orthodox Jews will assume that something went wrong in that person's life and that he or she "didn't *really* get the opportunity to truly learn Torah" and offer them support.

The exception may be when such a person is perceived as specifically and publicly targeting the community's values because Orthodox Jews realize that the formerly Orthodox Jew is well aware of Jewish law and the community's values and norms. For example, Jewish law prohibits driving a car on the Sabbath. If a non-Orthodox Jew does it, Orthodox Jews understand that the driver likely never even heard of this prohibition and even if the driver has, Orthodox Jews assume that he or she probably has no clue why it's considered wrong. However, if a formerly Orthodox Jew does it, Orthodox Jews find it upsetting because they know that he knows that it bothers the Orthodox community and is obviously driving through their community just to spite them. At the same time, there are still people in that community who will deal with that driver with compassion and understanding.

Orthodox Jews and Non-Jews

Orthodox Jews strongly desire to maintain cordial relations with the non-Jewish community. Some even have close non-Jewish friends. At the same time, some are wary of non-Jews. Some Orthodox Holocaust survivors, especially those who were betrayed to the Nazis by non-Jewish friends or neighbors, are distrusting of non-Jews and some communities are influenced by this view. And some Orthodox communities dwell among a non-Jewish population with a high crime rate, whose criminals target

Orthodox Jews. But even those who are wary of non-Jews do not attack non-Jews, not with physical violence nor with verbal abuse—unless, of course, in self-defense.

Orthodox Jews prefer it if non-Jewish or non-Orthodox men and women visit their communities dressed respectably. But they never expect a non-Jewish woman (or any unmarried woman) to cover her hair or for a non-Jewish man to wear a *kippah*. They don't consider non-Jews in any way obligated to follow Jewish laws. Non-Jews can eat their bacon double cheeseburger and talk about what a great time they had on the roller coaster last Saturday; Orthodox Jews don't really care.

Variations among Orthodox Jews

Orthodox Jews have their own slang, interweave Yiddish and Hebrew and Aramaic words into their English, dress differently (some more than others), and possess a different philosophy of life. Within the Orthodox community, people dress differently and even speak with mild yet prominent differences. For example, though they are both Ḥassidic, Lubavitcher women and Satmar women dress very differently. The differences are very obvious and Orthodox Jews can differentiate between a Lubavitcher woman and a Satmar woman at a glance. For example, Lubavitcher women cover their hair with stylish wigs while Satmar women wear elegant turbans.

General Lifestyle

Even the most sheltered Orthodox communities still offer the same amenities and services available anywhere else, but with an Orthodox twist. Depending on the size of the community, they'll provide, say, a state-of-the-art gym—but they'll have one for men and one for women. (Or separate hours for men and women.) And some of the women wear skirts (with maybe pants underneath) and hair-coverings when they work out in the all-female environment, while some wear pants with no skirt or even the latest style in gym clothes.

Orthodox institutions include universities and post-high school degree programs. If large enough, Orthodox communities can host restaurants, social services, stores of every type, and medical centers. They also offer quality schools that cater to special-needs children. Across the entire Orthodox spectrum, one finds doctors, lawyers, social workers, psychologists, occupational therapists, naturopaths, journalists, teachers, and scientists of both genders. Some Orthodox Jews are highly educated, extremely well-read, and multilingual, while at the opposite extreme, some can barely read English and are most proficient in speaking Yiddish (but may *read* classical Hebrew and Aramaic fluently).

Torah Learning

The importance of learning Torah to the Orthodox community cannot be understated. Religious studies alone make up about half the school day in Orthodox schools. Jewish law, Jewish thought, Jewish history, Biblical text with commentaries, ethical works—Orthodox Jews learn all this using the original Hebrew and Aramaic texts. After graduation, some men continue learning Torah full-time in a special type of institution called a *kollel* (KOH-lel). Some continue this way for a year or two, some several years, and some continue this way for their whole life.

Women learn Torah subjects in a post-high school institution called "seminary" (or "sem"). A variety of Orthodox seminaries and organizations around the world cater to women at all stages of life, academic levels, and religious backgrounds.

Orthodox communities offer Torah classes separately for both men and women and cover a wide range of subjects. People also get together for group-study or partnered study. Many people also have a daily learning schedule they carry out on their own. (This daily learning may range from anywhere between a few minutes to a few hours.) The primary goal is to polish up one's behavior and elevate one's inner potential by internalizing the learned values and ethics.

Language Differences

Due to the Ashkenazic majority, *frum* English is peppered with Yiddish terms, which are also adopted by *frum* Sefardic Jews, but those in Sefardic communities attending Sefardic schools will use fewer Yiddish terms and more Arabic or Hebrew terms.

Hebrew pronunciation varies, too. Ashkenazic Jews refer to the Jewish Sabbath as *Shabbos* while Sefardic Jews call it Shabbat. But Sefardic Jews in predominantly Ashkenazic communities will also say *Shabbos* and many Modern Orthodox Ashkenazic Jews say *Shabbat*.

Orthodox Jews naturally incorporate a lot of Hebrew, Yiddish, and Aramaic into everyday conversation.

For example:

"It was a total *nes* (Hebrew: miracle) that I managed to *shlep* (Yiddish: drag) all the kids to school on time *davka* (Aramaic: despite) after having been up all night with the baby." When the English is mixed with copious amounts of Yiddish, Hebrew, and Aramaic, it is colloquially known as "yeshivish English" or "yeshivish" or "frumspeak."

Yet another example is that among themselves, Orthodox Jews rarely use the English word "God," preferring instead a Hebrew term—*Hashem*—which literally means "The Name."

Naming Customs

Most Orthodox Jews have Hebrew or Yiddish names only, but some have English names that they use even within the Orthodox community. And by Hebrew name, I mean a Hebrew name with its original Hebrew pronunciation—like Yosef instead of Josef. Yakov instead of Jacob. Devorah instead of Deborah. Rivka instead of Rebecca. And then there are the cute nicknames: Yossi, Yanky (or Kobi), Devory, Rivki....

And some include an English name that has no relation to their Hebrew or Yiddish name, which they use for business and other dealings outside the Orthodox community. For example, Avraham may go by Andy.

Israel

Orthodox Jews feel very connected to Israel, both as a national and political entity and to the actual Land itself, which they hold to be innately holy. They truly believe that God designated the Land of Israel for the Jewish people and that giving this holy Land away, especially to terrorists, violates Jewish law and is spitting in God's Face (so to speak). Consequently, Orthodox Jews generally believe that Israel has a right to its own self-determination and self-defense. They are generally against a two-state solution, being very concerned about the numerous terror and missile attacks perpetuated against the Jewish people in Israel, the declared intention of Hamas to use a newly developed Palestinian state to destroy Israel or the PLO's declaration to "push Israel into the sea" or the so-called "moderate" Fatah's proclamation that "we will turn Tel Aviv into a ball of fire."

To Sum Up Orthodox Jews....

Just as in every single group throughout the world, you'll find within the Orthodox Jewish world energetic optimists, stern sticklers for rules, assertive go-getters, analytical academics, multi-tasking superstars, serene go-with-the-flow pacifists, introverts and extroverts, passionate idealists along with rigid conformists, poets and artists, and much more.

Conclusion & Suggested Resources

I hope the above descriptions have given you an idea of the complexity and diversity of American Jews—and have given you a window into how Judaism is experienced by different types of Jews. For more information about Judaism itself, you might find the following helpful:

Websites

www.torah.org

www.aish.com

www.talktogod.today/home.html

www.askmoses.com

www.simpletoremember.com

Books

Garden of Emuna by Rabbi Shalom Arush, translated by Rabbi Lazer Brody

The Universal Garden of Emuna by Rabbi Shalom Arush, translated by Rabbi Lazer Brody (this one is specifically for people who aren't Jewish and as per Jewish Law, it does NOT seek to convert people to Judaism)

The How, What and Why of Talking to God by Rivka Levy (available both as ebook and paperback)

Note: As of this printing, a free digital copy is available at: www.talktogod.today/free-ebook-sign-up.html

The Bible for the Clueless But Curious by Nahum Braverman

The Aryeh Kaplan Anthology by Aryeh Kaplan

Why Marry Jewish? by Doron Kornbluth

Outside/Inside by Gila Manolson

To be a Jewish Woman by Lisa Aiken

Faith and Fate: The Story of the Jewish People in the Twentieth Century by Rabbi Berel Wein

About the Author

To give you an idea of who wrote this book and where I'm coming from, here are a few words:

I was born in America to Conservative Jewish parents who, very lovingly and with the most wonderful of intentions, forced me to attend Conservative synagogue services, Hebrew school, and also Conservative Jewish summer camps. I liked the melodies of some of the prayers and also the fancy refreshments that followed the synagogue services, but was bored by everything else. I hated the thrice-weekly Hebrew school throughout elementary and junior high, but later felt profound gratitude for the firm grounding in Hebrew it gave me, along with some basics of Jewish prayer, belief, and songs—and most of the teachers were actually very good. Surprisingly, I enjoyed the once-a-week Hebrew high school (especially the classes taught by an Orthodox rabbi). Yet I absolutely hated the summer camps. Just totally, miserably hated them.

I attended public school, where I was usually one of two or three Jews in the entire school. In my teens, I became totally secular and unaffiliated (otherwise known as "just Jewish") even as my parents maintained a strong Conservative identity. While most of my friends were not Jewish, I did have a few Jewish friends who were Conservative, Reform, or—like me—totally secular and unaffiliated. Later, I became Modern Orthodox. And then I moved to Israel where I identified with the Religious Zionist community before finally settling into an ultra-Orthodox Sefardic identity, where I have happily remained.

Thanks so much for reading this book.

Dassie Dahan

www.dassiedahan-author.com

ACKNOWLEDGMENTS

I owe a tremendous debt of gratitude to God for all the unending good He has given and continues to give me.

I am also very grateful to all the wonderful Jews I met along the way who helped me get to where I am today.

I especially want to thank Rivka Levy of the Jewish Emotional Health Institute (www.spiritualselfhelp.org) for her inspiration and encouragement in writing and so much more.

And they don't know me, but I very much appreciate the generosity of successful writers such as Joanna Penn, Catherine Ryan Howard, and Eibhlin MacIntosh for all their generous guidance, both online and in print.

Glossary

Ashkenazi (Hebrew) – Jews who settled in Eastern Europe after the Exile from Israel

dati (Hebrew: dah-TEE) – religious

davka (Aramaic) – despite, in face of, just to spite

frum (Yiddish) – religious

Gemara (Aramaic) – a predominantly Aramaic elucidation of the Mishna

ḥaredi (Hebrew) ultra-Orthodox [literally, "one who trembles in wondrous awe before God"]

Hashem (Hebrew) – God [literally, "The Name"]

Ḥassidut/Ḥassidus (Hebrew/Yiddish) – a movement that developed among Eastern European Jews in the 1700s to renew the original Jewish passion and soul-connection to Torah Judaism

kasher (Yiddish) – to make something kosher

kashrut/kashrus (Hebrew/Yiddish) – the Jewish dietary laws

kippah (Hebrew) – that beanie that Jewish males wear on their heads

kolel (Hebrew) – a place where married Jewish men learn Talmud and Jewish law daily

kopel (Yiddish) – a kippah

Litvak (Yiddish) – a non-Hassidic Orthodox Jew [literally, "Lithuanian"; long ago, Lithuania was the spiritual hub of Torah learning for non-Hassidic Jews]

Mishna (Hebrew) – a Hebrew elucidation of the laws written in the Torah

misnagdim (Yiddish) – Jews who opposed the initial Ḥassidic movement

nes (Hebrew: nehss; Yiddish: nayss) – miracle

Rabbanit/Rebbetzin (Hebrew/Yiddish) – a rabbi's wife, but nowadays often used colloquially to mean a very learned female teacher or guide

Rav (Hebrew) – rabbi

Rebbe (Hebrew/Yiddish) – the leader of a Ḥassidic group

Sefardi (Hebrew) – Jews who settled in the Middle East, North Africa, and the Mediterranean after the Exile from Israel

Shabbat/Shabbos (Hebrew/Yiddish) – Saturday, the Jewish Sabbath

shlep (Yiddish) – to drag

shadḥan (Hebrew) – a matchmaker

shomer Shabbat/shomer Shabbos (Hebrew/Yiddish) – one who religiously observes all the laws pertaining to the Jewish Sabbath

Talmud (Hebrew) – a compilation of the Gemara and the Mishna, but often used interchangeably with the word "Gemara."

Torah (Hebrew) – Jewish Bible

yarmulke (Yiddish) – a *kippah*

yeshiva (Hebrew) – a place of Jewish learning

tav – almost the last letter of Hebrew alphabet: ﬨ

tav/thav/sav – the last letter of the Hebrew alphabet: ת

Index